Island Mindfulness

How To Use The Transformational Power Of Mindfulness To Create An Abundant Life

ISLAND MINDFULNESS:
HOW TO USE THE TRANSFORMATIONAL POWER OF MINDFULNESS TO CREATE AN ABUNDANT LIFE

Janet Autherine

Siblings, Janet Autherine James
& Mark Anthony Walker,
Jamaica, circa 1979

Copyright © 2020 by Janet Autherine

Autherine Publishing

Visit us on the Web at
www.JanetAutherine.com

ISBN: 978-0-9912000-2-3

Library of Congress Control Number: 2018905858

All rights reserved. No part of this publication may be reproduced, stored in a retrieval system, or transmitted in any form or by any means, electronic, mechanical, photocopying, recording, or otherwise copying (for commercial purposes), except for brief quotations in printed reviews, without the written consent of the publisher. To obtain permission, contact us at JanetAutherine@gmail.com.
Copyright © Janet Autherine.

Printed in the United States of America

June 2020

First edition

Island Mindfulness: How To Use The Transformational Power Of Mindfulness To Create An Abundant Life - A PART OF THE GROWING INTO GREATNESS SERIES OF INSPIRATIONAL BOOKS.

CONTENTS

INTRODUCTION

The Island That Made Me   8

PART 1:
Mindful Journey To Self-Empowerment   13

Don't Be Afraid to Take Flight   14
Love the Beautiful Person Who You Are Today   20
Be Mindful of Negative Thoughts and
Negative Influences   23
Let Your Intuition Be Your Guide   27
Negative News: Avoid This Limbo Dance   30
Sometimes "No Problem" Is a Problem:
Just Say "No" and Mean It   34
Everything in Moderation Except for Joy   38
Take a Mango! Nourishing Your Body and Your Soul   41

PART 2:
Mindful Journey To Meaningful Relationships   45

Mindful Living Starts with Family   46
Are You Ready to Have an Irie Time with Children?   50
Major Life Changes – Adjusting Your Sail   54
Don't Let Anyone Define Who You Are   58
Be the Captain of Your Sailboat   61
One Love: Grace in the Face of Prejudices   64

PART 3:
Mindful Journey To A Purposeful Life   69

Financial Abundance: Rich but Living a Rich
and "Irie" Life   70
Financial Abundance: Don't Shop with a Hole
in Your Basket   74
Include Your Heart when Choosing a Career   79
Strengths & Weaknesses: The Doctor Bird Flies
Backwards & the Parrot Speaks   82
Island Time: There is Joy in Being Patient   85
Procrastination or Mindful Delay   88
Death and Divorce: Rough Sea but Able Captain   91
Footprints in the Sand of Life   96

PART 4:
Mindful Journey To Spiritual Abundance   99

Flying High – Keep Your Mind Centered on Truth,
Not Fear   100
Connected Hearts and Hands   103
Emotional Fortitude: Strength of the Lignum Vitae   106
Let the Universe Guide your Journey   109
Legal and Moral Judgments: Enjoy the Sand but
Avoid the Sinkholes   112

PART 5:
Everything Is Irie: Lessons From The Journey 119

One Love, One Heart: Navigating Love and Marriage	120
Self-care is Life-care	127
Honoring our Roots: The Strength of a Woman	131
Lessons Learned from Taking the Long, Rugged but Scenic Drive Home	135
The Beginning and the End	140
EPILOGUE: The Poetry of Life – A Cottage on a Hill in Jamaica Overlooking the Ocean	143

About The Author   145

Moment Of Gratitude	146
Definitions	147
Acknowledgement	148

> *"Jamaica is more than just the 'brand' the world recognizes so well; it's a place of pride for the people who live here, its educational institutions, its sports achievements, its science and technology growth."*
>
> **PORTIA SIMPSON-MILLER**

The Island That Made Me

I grew up on the beautiful island of Jamaica and was raised in the small town of Dalvey, St. Thomas. I was raised in a household filled with love and kindness and struggle. I lived in a small house with my older brother, Mark, Ms. Linett, Granny Daw, Aunt Fan, Baba Joe, and Uncle Charlie. I loved them dearly; all the adults were over the age of 60 and were my village of elders. I didn't know their given names because we had informal names for everyone; I was Debbie or Debs until I moved to the United States and had to finally use the name 'Janet' on my birth certificate. When you share the same space with elders, you are sometimes called an "old soul." They were always giving advice and sharing their life experiences; and although I was busy being a carefree little girl, most of that advice resonated with me. I was socialized to listen, render advice, and solve problems. I always had a sense that the career I would choose would need to serve that innate instinct, or I would end up driving my friends and family crazy. Thankfully, as an introvert, I analyzed the issues that they shared, but most of the advice remained in my head.

Not everything was "Irie," but we made it so. We lived in a two-bedroom house with a rotating group of six relatives. We slept wherever we could find space and Ms. Linett often took in anyone who needed a place to stay short-term, so it was always a full house. We shared whatever food we had. "Community was vital to surviving and thriving. Community meant that your neighbor would help you with whatever you were lacking. I was surrounded by struggling but hardworking people who took pride in taking care of their surroundings and their families. We relied on education and hard work as our blueprint to a better life. Some of the things that my children would consider unusual were just part of my normal life—walking without shoes was normal; the "good shoes" were for special occasions. Walking a few miles to school or church with my friends was normal.

Jamaica is famous for the saying "No problem, mon." There are many problems, but we try to take them in stride. One frequently heard expression was: "What doesn't kill you makes you stronger." Jamaica has been hit with many storms, literally and figuratively but the people are strong and resilient and often find joy in the worst of circumstances. When storms come, there is devastation, but we always rely on the community to bounce back. The Island people, in general, have a reputation for being very laid-back—maybe it's the sun, our close relationship with the earth through planting and harvesting—or the sense that we have experienced tough times and joyous times and that you just have to get through the struggle to the victory of joy. You can still smile and be helpful in the midst of struggle and pain. It is that resilience that sparked the concept of island mindfulness.

We also treasure our leisure time; if you are the kind of person who likes to be in a rush, you will soon dislike the term "soon come" because it means; "I may be there this evening or tomorrow or later this week." Sometimes "Everything is Irie" is aspirational because the challenges we face are real and pressing, and that mindset has helped me get to the other side with an appreciation for the journey. While I would love to, I am not able to give my children the same childhood that I had because they are walking their own paths. However, I can pass on the lessons I have learned from my life growing up in Jamaica, as well as my journey as an immigrant in the United States.

Thanks for reading this book and allowing me to share my journey with you. I hope that some of my life lessons resonate with you, especially if you are young or young at heart and struggling to find peace in an often-frantic world. We all want an abundant life; for me, that means investing in self-empowerment, meaningful relationships, spiritual fulfillment and creating a purposeful life.

Friends, every moment of your journey is significant. I know that it can be a rough and winding road with lots of bumps along the way. But sometimes, we turn a corner and discover a majestic mountain that we are eager to climb or a beautiful lake that is inviting us to jump in. I don't know where you are on the journey but be mindful of every moment. We never get them back. Frankly, there are some moments we don't want to get back, but we always want to remember how far we have come. This book begins and ends with poetry because meditating and pouring my heart out on paper are the tools that I use to be mindful of each moment and to preserve the ones that are the most meaningful to me.

THE MOMENT IS OUR MAJESTY

*lean into each moment and let the transformation begin
island mindfulness brings the gift of presence
the convergence of a conscious mind and a free spirit
allows us to not be afraid to shout with
gladness and dance with joy
pouring like a river from our souls
on the high roads of life or
be vulnerable and show our hearts and
our humanity on the low roads
the freedom to be fully present for
this unpredictable journey
to deep dive into gratitude and take
every opportunity to foster
a meaningful connection with humanity–
seizing each moment
to love each other, be patient, emphatic
and kind to each other
lean into each moment because the moment is our majesty;
it is all that we are assured; the
universe giveth and taketh but
if we embrace the moment, the moment will embrace us.*

Island Mindfulness Mantras
Janet Autherine

LOVE
Each day, I create a legacy of love and service
I plant seeds of love for myself and my neighbors
I live in harmony with nature
I leave positive footprints in the sand for others to follow
My words and deeds are aligned

ABUNDANCE
I am enough
Love flows from within
The spirit within me will not pass this way again
I will manifest and embrace an abundant life and
continue to grow into greatness

PURPOSE
I walk in gratitude
I patiently work to discover my purpose and
I am mindful of each moment of the journey
I find meaning in the sun, wind & rain
When rain falls in my life, I embrace my humanity
and never lose sight of the divine

CONSCIOUSNESS
This is my moment, my journey.
I chose mindful living and being as my path
I am present for every step of the journey
I embrace Island Mindfulness so that
my mind and soul are at peace
and in my heart, everything is Irie

PART 1:
Mindful Journey To Self-Empowerment

ISLAND MINDFULNESS MANTRA
- ABUNDANCE

*I am enough
Love flows from within
The spirit within me will not pass this way again
I will manifest and embrace an abundant life and
continue to grow into greatness*

ISLAND MINDFULNESS: HOW TO USE THE TRANSFORMATIONAL
POWER OF MINDFULNESS TO CREATE AN ABUNDANT LIFE

www.janetautherine.com

"We are children of the world. Travel starts in our minds; we can visit all our "Irie" places and then command our feet to follow."

JANET AUTHERINE

Don't Be Afraid to Take Flight

My love for island hopping is why I am able to tap into the spirit of the islands and have been able to write this book. When I was younger, the only "vacation" that we could afford was going home to Jamaica. We just had to save for the airline ticket because we could stay with family. We couldn't return without gifts for our friends and relatives, so we would start buying reasonably priced items months before our trip. It felt so good to give love and receive love from the people who knew me best. I could speak "patwa" without confusing anyone, walk through the market on Saturday, go to the beach on Sunday, and feel completely loved and accepted in my own skin.

When I was able to afford to go on vacation, I always found myself asking the question, "Is there a beach there?" It didn't feel like a vacation without the island breeze and sand between my toes. My love for the islands has taken me to Barbados, the USVI (St. Thomas & St. John), the British Virgin Islands, Anguilla, Aruba, Hawaii, Puerto Rico, Trinidad and Tobago, the Dominican Republic, the Cayman Islands, and a few other islands through brief cruise stops. Saying that I felt at home doesn't seem to do the experience justice. I felt peace deep in my bones.

I have surrendered a small piece of myself wherever I have visited and have returned home with greater respect for the world and each of its cultures. I could fill a book discussing each island that I have visited but will share a few stories that have been particularly significant in my journey. I visited Barbados before I had children and was island and country hopping to visit as many carnivals as I could. There is no end to my love for Calypso and Soca music; my mother, Roslyn, played it in our house, and it seeped into my bones. Carnival in Barbados should be experienced by anyone who wants to feel joy in their bones. Barbados has some of the nicest people you will meet, and it comes alive at Carnival time. It was there that I fell in love with Allison Hinds, the queen of Soca. Watching her perform is watching beauty and joy in motion. On my first visit, I drove around the island in a day, but you wouldn't want to do this because there is so much beauty to see along the coast. The rough waters of the ocean beating against the rocks can keep you mesmerized for hours. I loved to sit and watch the waves and then stop on the way home to get bake and shark from a local vendor. Barbados revealed to me the diversity of the Caribbean experience and taught me that I didn't need to rush. It was ok to live in the moment and sit and watch the waves all day if it brought me joy.

I have visited Puerto Rico a few times and simply love the island. San Juan is magical at night, and there is so much beauty to explore when you venture inland. We rented a car and drove around the island. The further inland we went, the less English could the beautiful islanders that we met understood. I learned that the universal language when traveling is a smile and food; everyone understands a discussion about food. My last visit to Puerto Rico was the most memorable because we managed to get lost in the El Yunque National Forest. The rainforest is magical, and we were happily enjoying its beauty when we lost track of the trail. That it was also raining, didn't improve matters. After walking seemingly in circles, panic set in. I learned a few things from that trip. First, no good decision can be made when your mind is in a panic. Second, fear is normal and can protect you. We often tell each other not to be afraid, but there are times when fear is legitimate. Thankfully, we met a couple who were also lost, and we found our way out together; sometimes a problem is much less frightening when you realize that you are not alone. Amidst an emergency or uncertainty, be still, read the map, assess the situation—think about how you steered off the path and how you can get back on it. This is also true for the misadventures of life.

I was in the US Virgin Islands when I was almost eight months pregnant and feeling very vulnerable. I was insecure about my size, worried about getting seasick, and slightly afraid that the baby would come early. I was suffering from fibroids, and sometimes they would get into fights with the baby, causing earth-shattering pain. I pushed aside my fears to travel because I felt that everything in my life would change in a few weeks and I needed the island breeze to calm my nerves and ground me for the changes to come. I explored St. Thomas, St. John and the British Virgin Islands and enjoyed the diversity of each island. St. Thomas was a fast-paced, shopper's paradise with the ocean only steps away. St. John was so tranquil that I wanted to pitch a tent on the beach and never leave; the pace of life on the British Virgin Islands was the perfect depiction of island mindfulness. Everything moved at the rate of its own heartbeat and not a second faster. I was too young to fully appreciate the beauty of that stillness but that has changed into a full appreciation for mindfulness. I met some new friends in St. Thomas—Iguanas! They were everywhere, extremely friendly, and inspired fear. I love nature and have a strong respect for the natural inhabitants of any space; it is beautiful when humans and nature intersect and can live together peacefully, but I can still feel the panic I felt when I discovered an iguana using my beach towel. I am hoping that on my next visit, I will be able to enjoy a symbiotic relationship with them.

My fear inspired the poem, "Sister Nature," which I wrote on the flight back home.

SISTER NATURE

Snakes, Iguanas, alligators
Inspire fear for just being
beautiful, carefree, alive
Surviving, thriving in shared space
Feared, fearing in shared space
Your freedom, my freedom intertwined
Both looking to be
Free
To share this land of liberty

Writing is empowering. Wherever the journey takes me, there is a story to share that will teach, motivate, or empower. What empowers you? What inspires you to take flight?

Island Mindfulness

Traveling makes you feel like you are one with the world. It reminds you that your world is larger than the country that you were born in. That the same blood runs through all our veins, that a child in the small town of Drapers in Jamaica is just as important as a child born in Manhattan. It reminds us that we all face the same issues but that some of us are fortunate enough to have the resources to face those challenges. The most liberating lesson for me is that you don't have to grow where you were planted. Your view of life can be quite different depending on where you are standing. You can move across the street, retire in Costa Rica, take the family for a drive every Sunday to the beach, go on a study-abroad trip, travel with the Peace Corps, or go on a mission trip with your church. There is a way for everyone to step out of the box they were born in—even when constrained by time and finances. As someone who was born into poverty, the Sundays when we went to the beach were incredibly special. I suspect that my deep attachment to beaches stemmed from witnessing the vastness of the ocean and believing that anything is possible. Take the time needed to meditate on what have been the driving forces in your life, thus far? In that space, you will find the tools to spread your wings, step outside the box and take flight in all areas of your life.

> "If you have no confidence in self, you are twice defeated in the race of life."
>
> **MARCUS GARVEY**

Love the Beautiful Person Who You Are Today

Self-love is not a waiting game. Who are you today, and how can you honor that person with love, support, and self-acceptance amid struggle, confusion, lost loves, career shifts, health crises and all the beauty and complications of life? We never reach perfect perfection; we are just perfectly imperfect people that are fabulous in our complexities.

I have been that island girl running barefoot in her yard, the confused immigrant trying to navigate primary school in a new country with her very strong Jamaican accent, and the African-Caribbean-American student trying to find her identity and place on the college campuses of Penn State University and Boston College Law School. I have been the introvert trying to figure out how to function as a lawyer when I hate meetings, small talk, and being in the spotlight. I have been the "living life like it's golden" girl—restaurant hopping, Caribbean carnival seeking, free-spending, with a live-and-let-live spirit. Speaking of Carnival seeking, I have played mass for two days in Trinidad in full costume, going two days without sleep to enjoy the festivities, and I have been to Carnival in Jamaica and Barbados, and I have taken road trips to almost every city in the United States (Miami, NY, Baltimore, DC, Atlanta) and Canada (Caribana) that had a carnival. Most of us can't be placed in a box, although society tries awfully hard to do so.

I appreciated being the carefree 20-something, the career-driven young adult just looking for the next ladder to climb—and now, the single mother of three boys. My mission is to try to manage home life and work-life as an administrative law judge without losing all my hair and finding some time for my writing, which has always been my passion. I have fallen many times and struggled to find my way back up, but with each fall, you learn that you are strong and resilient and love and appreciate yourself a bit more. Be grateful for every step on your journey and always root for yourself.

SELF-ACCEPTANCE

is a journey from
will they like me to
will i like them to
i am who i am
no judgment
no affirmation needed
i am enough.

Island Mindfulness

Eventually, you get to the point in life where you declare: I am who I am, I love me, and there isn't much, if anything, that I want to change about myself. I am open to personal growth, but I fully embrace where I am on my journey. Wow! The road to this type of confidence and self-acceptance is usually long and rocky. Along this road, try to be mindful of every step, be kind and forgiving to yourself. See each mistake as an opportunity to learn more about yourself and the world. Use your mistakes as stepping stones to a higher place, and celebrate every victory—both the ones that you labored for and the ones that the universe blessed you with. Don't compare yourself to others because no one else is on the same journey. Most importantly, love who you are today!

> *"You're not supposed to feel down over whatever happens to you. I mean, you're supposed to use whatever happened to you as some type of upper, not a downer."*
>
> **BOB MARLEY**

Be Mindful of Negative Thoughts and Negative Influences

Most of us can relate to fear and self-doubt on some level. It is the root cause of negative thoughts and behavior. Although I am an optimist, I have my challenges. If someone starts talking about the flu, I start to feel that I am on the verge of catching the flu myself. I used to constantly check on the children at night, and I have driven all the way home just in case, God forbid, I have forgotten to turn the iron off and might come home to a burning house.

Sometimes, having negative thoughts is a normal mechanism that serves to keep us safe—i.e., don't cross the street until the light is green as you may become the next breaking news story. Some affect us only minimally—we don't go bungee jumping because we can see ourselves plummeting, or we encourage our children not to play football because the potential for injury is high or we don't ask the stranger across the room to dance because a little voice tells us that the risk of rejection is high. While some optimists would encourage us to picture ourselves soaring to new heights as we bungee jump, picture our children injury-free and holding the Super Bowl trophy, or discovering that the girl across the room is our soul-mate—I think most of us can live with the label of "cautiously" optimistic. However, if pessimism, negative thinking, and cynicism seep into your mind and soul, and your actions and reactions are guided by it, then you have to admit that is it time to try and change your wiring.

Most negative preoccupation is driven by fear. The first is the kind that holds us back from achieving a goal; it can generally be described as a lack of confidence in oneself. It is losing the race long before we even enter the game. The second is fatalistic thinking. We don't want to fly because the airplane may crash, or we don't want to send our children to the pool because we fear that they may drown. We wouldn't go on a roller coaster because we see it as a death trap, we wouldn't dare go skiing because that can only result in broken bones. In short, we live in fear and see accidents happening all around us.

Similarly, negative influences chip away at our emotional reserve. Is there someone in your life that is always feeding you negativity and it is draining to you? There are always a million things going wrong in their lives at any given time, and they can't wait to tell you about them all. They call you to share every bit of gossip and keep you up to speed on every way in which the world is falling apart around you and them. Upon further inquiry, you realize that their struggles are no different from the ones you and your other friends are dealing with—but these friends refuse to be helped or consoled—preferring instead to reside in that negative space. Generally, it takes many months of trying to help before you realize or admit to yourself that this beloved friend is one that simply refuses to allow herself to be happy. Sadly, this means that out of sheer self-preservation, you have to pull back and become less invested in the friendship. Always be mindful of the impact your words may have before you set them free—both to others and to yourself. Your inner thoughts should be rooting for you to succeed in every area of your life. Also, don't allow yourself to become that negative energy in someone else's life.

FREE YOUR MIND

Be mindful of negativity
Negative thoughts become obsessions
Obsessions become deep emotions
Emotions become painful
Pain becomes cancerous to the body
Free the mind from poison

Island Mindfulness

Although we may not realize it, when we are in a negative state of mind, we are radiating and conveying negative energy, and it affects us internally, as well as the way others perceive us. It stops us from living our best life or walking boldly into our purpose. You are not walking boldly if your feet are weighed down by fear. Mindfulness forevermore asks, am I traveling light today? What is weighing me down and how can I unload it constructively? If negative thoughts, news, and people are weighing you down, free yourself; it's easier to face the challenges of life if you are traveling light.

> *"We don't achieve every dream, but we achieve every dream that is aligned with our destiny. If you are standing on the deck watching your sailboat leave, trust that you were not meant for that journey."*
>
> **JANET AUTHERINE**

Let Your Intuition Be Your Guide

We all have an inner compass, regardless of our age. Wisdom comes with age, but our inner compass or intuition starts at birth. It's that general sense that things will be ok, that we are moving in the right direction, or it's that gut feeling that something is really wrong, even in times when we can't identify what it is.

When I was in high school, finding a summer job was very challenging. One summer, I was in North Philadelphia when I spotted a flyer offering summer jobs for high school students. I called the phone number and the man on the telephone suggested that we meet for an interview—and if all went well—he would drive me to the job site. I suggested conducting the interview at a public hospital that was convenient for both of us. It just didn't feel like we were working in the confines of a traditional interview situation, but I was young and wasn't certain. I did have enough sense to take a male friend with me to the meeting. If it seemed legitimate, he would wait for me in the car. As planned, I met the interviewer but when I mentioned that I had someone with me, he excused himself and didn't return. I am quite certain that I escaped a possible kidnapping or some other nefarious activity. I've learned to trust my instincts and err on the side of being too cautious. Sometimes, it is better to risk missing an opportunity than walk a path that feels like it may be leading in the wrong direction.

Our inner compass can keep us out of many problematic situations. For instance, we all have a natural sense of right and wrong. We get an uncomfortable feeling just before we tell what we consider to be a white lie (that dress looks great on you) or we break a rule, even if it seems insignificant (don't bring that food into the movie theater even if the popcorn there is overpriced). If your friends want to go skating in the pond and you suddenly hesitate, take a minute to explore why. Is the feeling born from fear, insecurity about your skating ability or is your intuition telling you that the ice is unsafe?

Island Mindfulness

Our inner compass is the thing that keeps us on the right path when our actions or words are about to be out of sync with our values. Get to know that feeling, go with your gut, follow your inner compass and most of the time you won't be led astray. Sometimes, we are afraid to trust our instincts because we don't want to be embarrassed. If you live in the United States, many of the security warnings have the slogan, "If you see something, say something." Many of us are afraid to do so because we don't trust our instincts, we think someone else is a better judge of the situation, or we don't want to be mistaken and end up on the evening news for all the wrong reasons. Get to know yourself and your inner motivations so that you can trust your intuition. Take a mindful minute to assess each situation and then make a decision from a place of strength.

> "I am good. I live good. I think good.
> I don't have to feel good to be good; I
> take my goodness wherever I go."
>
> **PETER TOSH**

Negative News: Avoid This Limbo Dance

I love art that entertains, and I usually enjoy being well-versed on whatever artistic expression is trending in our society. However, I have skipped watching a few of the most fun or acclaimed shows—The Walking Dead, Breaking Bad, and Game of Thrones, just to name a few. How could I? Part of the reason is that I cut back on television to write but it was also because I was in a space that didn't allow me to absorb too much negative energy from the outside. I was going through a divorce, navigating being a single parent, fretting over the inability to stay afloat financially. There was enough stress and drama in my life that I could only let in positive energy—comedies, musicals, talent shows. For most of my life, witnessing a murder on Law and Order, Scandal, and The Blacklist didn't affect me because it was just acting; however, in the midst of my own drama, I didn't find drama manufactured for entertainment entertaining.

Know what causes your spirit to soar and what causes it to want to bury your head in the sand and hide. For me, it is the negative news cycle. I try to avoid movies with gratuitous violence, scary plotlines or particularly disturbing topics, such as the death or abuse of a child. I know myself well enough to know that this does not entertain me; it creates tension in my bones that lingers with me throughout the night and sometimes for days. Why subject my mind, body, and soul to such assault? When I do watch television, I limit myself to no more than an hour per day. Most news stories can be wrapped up in half an hour. The rest is repetitive and mostly negative. It seems as if every news segment starts with a death or a story about someone else's misfortune. Over time, our hearts become hardened and desensitized, and we may even become voyeuristic and excited by the drama that is unfolding.

Reading is my avenue to staying engaged without becoming overwhelmed. I scan the headlines for content that is important to my daily life and read just the facts. I get to avoid all the unnecessary dramatic commentary, disturbing photos, and the constant "breaking news." Reading allows the mind to process information at a speed that it can handle without becoming overwhelmed. A good writer can write a crime scene quite violently, but it is rarely as jarring to the senses as the same scene adapted for a movie audience.

ABOVE IT ALL

Today, I forgot to breathe
The air was suspended between my throat and nose
Frozen in anticipation of news of war and death
Famine and starvation
Rape and murder

Pride and pain
Fear and gridlock
Spam and debt
Depression and loneliness
Sadness and tears

Tomorrow, I will turn off the radio, the television,
the internet, negative people

I will take flight above the clouds
Where the air is thin and
I don't have to remind myself to breathe
Catching glimpses of life as it crashes by
Descending only when I am focused on
each breath, each heartbeat, each emotion
And everything that has meaning.

Island Mindfulness

What is polluting your mind? You have the power to change the climate in your mind. Stand up for yourself, set boundaries, and limit interactions with negative events that your mind surely will absorb. Change the channel, read, meditate, and find other ways to protect your mind and soul. There is positive energy everywhere, but we have to seek it. If you are on social media, follow websites that promote positivity so that your screen isn't filled with everything bad that happened that day. Avoid social media first thing in the morning or right before you go to sleep. Start and end the day with good energy. Although we are all surrounded by negative energy, you are in control of what your mind absorbs. Don't abdicate that control. Be mindful of what is absorbed into your mind and soul. All the abundance around you cannot be enjoyed if your mind is under siege. Joy is something that can be stolen—so don't leave the door open for the thieves to come in.

> *"Remember that you are more powerful than you think. Wake up. Stay awake. Stand tall and be courageous. You are strong enough to speak your truth! No apologies needed."*
>
> **JANET AUTHERINE**

Sometimes "No Problem" Is a Problem: Just Say "No" and Mean It

Jamaicans are known for saying "no problem" to most requests; it is our way of saying that anything is possible and if it is possible, we can get it done. One of the most important lessons to learn is where to allocate your time and energy. To do so effectively requires learning to say "no" to the things that deplete you mentally and physically and say "yes" to things that advance your goals or bring you joy. Seems easy, right? Then why is it so hard to say no? Why is such a tiny word so difficult to utter? For me, it was always the fear of causing disappointment. "No" is a tiny word, but disappointment is a pretty big and emotionally weighty word. Also, the word "no" rarely stands alone; often, long, and uncomfortable explanations are required. Then there are the arguments and counterarguments. Often, it's just easier to say "yes." "No" is even harder to say when you think that you have no "good" reason. It took me a long time to have the inner confidence and self-assurance to say "no" just because

I didn't feel like doing something or going somewhere. It has taken me years to achieve this confidence, but I no longer feel the need to come up with an explanation that would be palatable to someone else. Let me share a few bumps along that journey.

When I think of my childhood, I think of kindness; it was one of the strongest virtues in my household, and it is even more important to me now that I am raising my own children. I initially confused kindness with being accommodating, even when it was to my own detriment. If it was possible to say "yes" to a request, I did, even if it required tying myself in knots to accomplish the task. I have learned that that type of kindness is not kind and it's not charitable, and it can build resentment. A friend would ask for a loan, and instead of telling the truth and saying "I am sorry, but I don't have it to lend," I would borrow from my rent payment or tuition payment and then cross my fingers and hope that I would get it back in time to meet my own obligations. If I had a bad date, instead of saying, "No, I just don't think that we are right for each other," and end the conversation, I would say it was fine or invent reasons why I was too busy to go out again. With technological advancements, daters just "ghost" each other, but there was actually a time when breakups required a phone call or a difficult face-to-face discussion.

Have you ever sat through a timeshare presentation, bought a car, or another large purchase because you felt pressured and didn't know how to exit the situation? For some reason, all the self-empowerment that we learn seems to get lost in those situations. I often stay away from car showrooms, jewelry stores, electronics stores, and any store where a salesperson invests more than 10 minutes showing me a product. Many times, I have walked out of a store with a dress that the salesperson loved, but I only liked, or a handheld vacuum that I didn't need and couldn't afford because I was overcome by an enthusiastic sales job and couldn't muster the strength to say "no" after the salesperson had "invested" so much time in me. Well, the presentation was not about me; it was about a commission, and it was tailor-made to target every customer walking in the door. If you want to practice the art of saying no, try sitting through a timeshare presentation? I have done so many times over, and I won't spend more than 30 minutes in one ever again; the free dinner coupon is not worth the overwhelming sales pressure. However, if you truly did not like or could not afford the product, and you had the mental fortitude to walk away under such extreme pressure, you can likely say no to any other decision in life that does not align with your purpose. Saying "no" if it is your truth, is the kindness way to interact with someone. Often, we are caught off guard by a question and don't know what the answer should be. In that case, it is perfectly ok to say, "Please, give me some time to think about that, and I will get back to you." If you get pressured for an answer, then say, "Since there is no time to think about it, my answer will have to be 'no.'"

HUMANITY NOT FOR SALE

you are worthy
always have been
i see you
giving, serving, loving
until your cup is empty
fueled by the need to please
letting the takers of the world take
until you are hollow on the inside
it is time to reclaim your humanity
chant, I am worthy, always have been
there is nothing else for me to prove
i am more than enough
it is time for me to exhale and just BE.

Island Mindfulness

Be mindful of that uneasy feeling that you get when you are about to say, "yes" but mean "no." If you feel uneasy about a decision—any decision—sleep on it, walk away until you stop sweating and that feeling in the pit of your stomach disappears. I think of that feeling as common sense kicking in and our intuition telling us that we are out of our comfort zone as a warning to tread carefully. I am also teaching my kids to have great respect for the word "no" in their personal lives and social situations. When you hear it, take it seriously. A "no" is not a "maybe" and it is never a "yes." Every "no" to things that we don't love is empowering and it creates room for saying "yes" to things that contribute to an abundant life.

> "Live and love in perfect harmony with the universe. The universe is rarely emotional, but when it is joyful or tearful, the earth shakes."
>
> **JANET AUTHERINE**

Everything in Moderation Except for Joy

I believe in moderation; it is not sexy or groundbreaking, but it has kept me grounded. There are things that we should never do, for starters, anything illegal or harmful to your mental or physical health (insert your own list here because I wouldn't jump out a perfectly good airplane, but I won't judge others who would), but most things are great when done in moderation. During college, I had the great fortune of going on a study abroad trip to Westminster, England. It was a rich, thrilling educational experience that I will never forget, and I encourage every college student to add study abroad programs as a part of their educational journey. When you are exploring the world, you follow the lead of the locals, so one of our first stops was the pub. The British are known for their love of a good drink at the pub and sharing cheers with friends. After six weeks of the pub tour, it lost its charm; there was no more joy in it. This was a blessing for me because it allowed me to fully enjoy and remember all my days and nights in college. While some friends tell alcohol-fueled party stories, the stories that I tell about college involve working at the post office, going to Nittany Lion football games, and very tame partying with my friends in the Caribbean Students Association.

Even the things that are good for us, like food, love, and music, require moderation so that we have time to navigate life and achieve our goals. I used to watch television for several hours each day, but my mother kept reminding me that the actors on television are working and have already been paid—so I needed to reduce my consumption and focus on my own goals. I am now the mother and I find myself passing on the same lessons to my children. When I found myself repeatedly saying that I didn't have the time to write, I knew in my heart that it wasn't true so I gave up watching television for over a year, used the time to write and wrote two books and many poems. Sometimes, moderation results in abundance.

Obviously, moderation does not apply to harmful behavior, such as abuse, racism, or other forms of hate. I struggled to think of something that was not better in moderation, and the only thing that I could come up with is JOY. A joy that makes you smile from the inside out, lights up your soul and makes you realize that every bit of life is worth living.

Island Mindfulness

Name five things that you love; they should be things that come to mind immediately. If you are laboring over the answer, place the item in the "like" pile. For me, it is books, music, hugs, mangoes, and quiet time to reflect and recharge. Music and books were the best friends of this introvert island girl. In Jamaica, we lived below a shop that in addition to selling goods, also played music and was an informal center for the community. I spent many evenings sitting on my front stoop listening to the sounds of the Honorable Robert Nesta Marley, Jimmy Cliffy and other reggae greats. When I moved to Philadelphia, I repeatedly played the few albums that we had in the house—Kenny Rogers, Abba, and Engelbert Humperdinck.

Sit for a moment and meditate on these questions—who do you call when you have great news? What would you grab if your house was on fire? What source of pleasure would you engage in excessively if it was legal or if it wouldn't harm you? Is there something in your life that could use some moderation? If the things that you love have the potential to be harmful, such as gambling, wine, or shopping, this answer is important because you have just identified where your vulnerability lies, and this is the first step to avoiding a pitfall. These are temporary pleasures, not joy. Likewise, by identifying the things that are authentic to your experience and are a positive source of joy, you know what abundance means to you. During challenging times, these things can be your anchor.

> *"Good food and good love are cultivated the same way – plant a seed in fertile soil, water it, care for it daily, protect it from negative elements and watch it rise up to nourish your body and soul."*
>
> **Janet Autherine**

Take a Mango! Nourishing Your Body and Your Soul

Eat healthily, eat well, and sometimes just eat something that you love. Food is not just for the body; it is for the mind, and it awakens all of our senses when the ingredients and presentation conspire to excite us. Our ultimate goal is to live a long and healthy life without the need for numerous medications and medical procedures. This is an area where moderation matters; we don't want to have lived a long life but felt so deprived throughout that we didn't enjoy any of it—nor do we want to indulge in everything that excites us but die early or live on medications. We are what we put into our bodies, and many illnesses and deaths are at least partially attributed to food, they are just given different names: diabetes, cancer, heart disease.

Understanding that we are what we eat, my diet primarily consists of vegetables, herbal teas, a very limited amount of pasta and rice, fish (but no other meat) and lots of fruit. I have tried quite a few diets, including the vegan diet. Veganism is a great way of life if it is right for your body type and you are able to have a healthy mind, body, and soul as a vegan. For me, giving up fish and the occasional piece of cheese didn't result in a positive mind/body balance. I agree that dairy is not good for the body, and neither are most meats, especially if they are not organic. The right choice for me is to be a 90% dairy-free pescatarian. As an islander, fishing is a big part of our culture and a healthy part of our diet. I don't purchase dairy products for my home, but I also don't feel guilty about having a small cube of cheese at a professional wine and cheese event or having a small dessert at a restaurant that contains dairy.

While pregnant with Gabriel, I gave up processed foods and ate mostly organic vegetables. During that time, I went to a conference in Jamaica and threw the diet out of the window. I decided to indulge in island delicacies without regard for calorie or fat content. For breakfast, I had dumplings and yams and ackee and saltfish; for lunch, I had red snapper with rice and peas, and for dinner, I had a large lobster with potatoes. Sometimes, it's worth it to break a few rules. Clearly, this was not about what my stomach needed; it was about what my mind and my soul needed. During that trip, I needed to revert to all the wonderful foods that were a staple in my diet as a child.

Island Mindfulness

Be mindful of what you eat because it will either heal or harm you. If it is processed, filled with unnatural ingredients, and laden with calories from unhealthy fats, it is going to harm, not heal. I sometimes try a mental reality check—in a few hours, will I be thankful that I didn't eat this or cry because I missed out on a delicacy or unique meal? Eat healthy every day but don't hesitate to try something new during a vacation or have cake at your child's birthday party. When I visited Ghana and Senegal, I tried almost every local dish that was presented, especially the stews. Have a healthy relationship with food. Don't substitute food for emotional comfort, but don't be afraid to live a little. Find something new and healthy to try each month. Try a trip to a Caribbean market and try guava, avocado, cerasse tea, ackee, jerk sauce, coconut water without additives, or a soursop!

PART 2:

Mindful Journey To Meaningful Relationships

ISLAND MINDFULNESS MANTRA
- LOVE

Each day, I create a legacy of love and service
I plant seeds of love for myself and my neighbors
I live in harmony with nature
I leave positive footprints in the sand for others to follow
My words and deeds are aligned

ISLAND MINDFULNESS: HOW TO USE THE TRANSFORMATIONAL
POWER OF MINDFULNESS TO CREATE AN ABUNDANT LIFE

www.janetautherine.com

> "In hindsight, I see the great value of family and how it molded my life and kept me together. So now family means everything to me."
>
> **JIMMY CLIFF**

Mindful Living Starts with Family

Abundance for me means an abundance of love; it means having meaningful relationships with friends and family. Every summer, we take a family road trip. Most of my wonderful family memories are from these trips. I love the closeness that we experience as a family when we are on the road. One year, we drove from Orlando to Martha's Vineyard, making stops in Savannah, GA, Charleston, SC, Richmond, VA, Washington, DC, and New York. As you may guess, there were a lot of "Are we there yet?" moments on that 1300-mile trip. But we had no electronic entertainment in the SUV, so we had to entertain each other. The kids looked out the window and asked questions about everything from the mundane (the speed of cars passing us by) to thoughtful questions (the histories of all the churches in South Carolina).

When we traveled, we usually stayed in a single room or a one-bedroom apartment. We all shared the same small bed; it just felt right to be in such close proximity to the family. I loved to hear Gian breathe as he slept. These are the small things that we take for granted on a daily basis. The kitchen was usually in the same space as the living room, so we could have a conversation that involved the entire family as I washed the dishes or cooked. In these close quarters, we felt like more of a family than we have ever felt in our spacious house. I used to think that it would be great to have a larger house with another bedroom. Traveling changed my perspective; I felt that we had too much space, and I thought about how nice it would be to have the boys share a bedroom and share stories? If we were back home, the kids would be playing in their rooms or watching television upstairs, and I would be in the kitchen or my office. I would definitely give up a room or two to consistently feel the closeness that we feel on our vacations.

GRATEFUL HEART – A MOTHER'S POEM OF THANKSGIVING

For my children, I give thanks.
When you were born, the universe smiled on me.
Your love is unconditional; my love is unconditional.
You are a joy. You are hope. You are home.
My walking heartbeats.

Every day, you stand taller in height and heart.
When you smile, I smile.
I smile because of your kind spirit
Your pure heart. Your innocence.
Your never-ending search for fun.

Continue to grow into your greatness.
Always hopeful. Always kind.
Always grateful. Always loving.
No pomp, circumstance or occasion needed.
Every day with you is Thanksgiving Day.

Island Mindfulness

Be mindful of how you allocate your time. If you ask anyone what is most important to them, the answer will likely be family. But we often take the ones that we love for granted. We assume that they will always be there. If priority is defined by time spent, our priority is our work. On an average day, we hurriedly get through our morning routine and maybe spend a very rushed hour before work with our loved ones. We then work for eight hours and get home around dinner-time to rush through the evening routine of dinner and dishes while we watch the news. If we are fortunate, we get to sit down with the family for dinner, or to watch television, or to do homework together for about an hour, and then everyone is off to bed. Many parents still have to work on weekends; however, do your best to squeeze in some quality family time. Having at least some family time every week is a necessity. My mother worked three jobs to take care of us, so I understand the grind. However, we could see her hard work and dedication to her family and knew that we were loved. When we found time to connect, it was meaningful.

When you do get time with family, live in the moment, and make every moment with your loved ones count. Say, 'I love you' through words and deeds, and remind everyone that they matter. If you are often working, remind the family why you are away so often; don't assume that they automatically understand. Create moments of love, laughter, and togetherness over food, games, music, or whatever is important in your culture.

> "I have a career, which is important, but my family is the priority. First, family, and then career. It's a delicate balance."
>
> **JIMMY CLIFF**

Are You Ready to Have an Irie Time with Children?

Children are a joy and an enormous blessing, but so is having time to write, lazy Sunday afternoons with nothing on the agenda, relaxing evenings watching your favorite guilty pleasure, sports cars with no baby seat, and bachelor pads without several child safety gates. And how about breasts that don't sag from nursing, that extra $2,000 now going to daycare and diapers, weekly nights out with the girls, and a movie that doesn't have Elmo in them. If you are reading this and you think, "No big deal! I have enjoyed all those things, and I'm ready for the next phase of my life," then congratulations, you may be ready to become a parent.

I realized that my definition of "fun" had to be adjusted when the family attempted to take a leisurely Sunday afternoon trip. I spent 30 minutes in the garage nursing the baby who was crying, while my older son screamed to get out the car. After a few minutes in the stroller, Gian declared that he wanted to walk and sulked when we wouldn't let him out. At the ice cream store, I purchased a smoothie for myself and a cup of vanilla ice cream for Gian who took a few licks and decided that he wanted my smoothie instead. My food was no longer my own. As there were no seats in the store, we stood by the window and ate. On the way back to the car, I attempted to get a magazine from the bookstore. Giorgio started to cry and wanted to be picked up and then Gian started to scream because if Giorgio was getting out of the stroller, he wanted to get out too. I had to end my search for the magazine and usher us out of the bookstore so that everyone else at the magazine rack could enjoy their browsing. We all went back to the car, I fed Giorgio again, and we were on our way back home. Compared to previous attempts, which was a "fun" outing—it seemed that "fun" had been redefined.

The truth is that parents don't really lower their expectations, they just change them. For every mind-numbing outing, there are a hundred mind-blowing moments with the kids.

It is challenging to change your expectations and still be happy unless you have lived enough to be ready to put the needs of the children first. It is easy to make this transition when you have enjoyed all the seasons of your life. Looking back at all my seasons, I wish that I enjoyed them more, but I have no major regrets. I enjoyed the college years, the law school years, the anxious, but fun early 20s, the "what I am going to do with my life" late 20s. Most of the things that I am missing out on now, I can look back and say to myself that I have been there and done that. Partying: check. Concerts: check. Girls' getaways: check. Career: check. With those boxes checked, it was easier to relax and enjoy the beauty of the toddler years.

I wrote this poem during an anxiety-filled time in my life. I had three boys in diapers and the toddler years were challenging. This poem was an attempt to exhale and appreciate the beauty in my journey.

TODDLER

*The passengers hurry by you on the airplane,
afraid to sit next to your delightful presence.*

*The shoppers give you dirty looks in the supermarket
as you enjoy the racetrack called the supermarket aisle.*

*The diners stare as you empty the saltshaker on
the dinner table to satisfy your curiosity.*

*The museum workers give you stern looks as you
scream in delight at the beauty of the artwork.*

*The church members are surprised as you clap and
loudly sing the hymn of praise.*

*You are my toddler. Pure uncensored joy,
boundless energy, and unlimited curiosity become you!*

Island Mindfulness

Before you decide to have children, it is important to know that you don't have to have children. You are not letting society down; you are still a wonderful person. It's fine not to have maternal or paternal instincts, you will still be fine in your old age, and you are not selfish. Society places so much pressure on us, especially women to get married and procreate that we have to be mindful of our motivations and be sure that the decision that we are making is for the right reasons.

The decision to have children is one of the most important, life-changing decisions that you will ever make. It requires deep soul searching and a deep understanding of yourself. Be mindful of where you are in your journey. Are you ready to live a life of service to tiny human beings? Are there still professional and personal goals that you would like to achieve before having children? You may want to accomplish the important ones so that you are not parenting with a spirit of regret or resentment. Are you financially stable? Do you have a supportive partner or a supportive family? Parenting alone can be a very lonely and overwhelming experience. If you answered "yes" to these questions, then you are in the parenting zone. Welcome to one of the most rewarding rides of your life.

> *"You never know how strong you are,
> until being strong is your only choice."*
>
> **BOB MARLEY**

Major Life Changes – Adjusting Your Sail

After the birth of my first son, Gian, I took two months of maternity leave. I became a new mom and made the transition from being completely career-focused to creating a more balanced life. It sounds wonderful on paper but it was very challenging in practice. It was very challenging to shift from a person who lives by a to-do-list to someone whose day is completely controlled by a newborn. Before the baby, I would start the day by either reviewing yesterday's checklist or starting a new one. The more things that I accomplished during the day, the more successful I felt at the end of the day.

After the baby, I was now confused as to how to define success because there was no concept of day and night—at least not for the little one. Sleep was rare; my days consisted of sitting on the sofa and nursing constantly. I referred to myself as the milk lady. All the multitasking that I anticipated was out the window. I was initially afraid to leave the house alone with the baby. My biggest accomplishment was taking him for a walk three blocks from my house. It took me more than three hours and all the stars aligning to help me accomplish that walk because every time I made it to the door, I had to nurse again or change another diaper.

After a few weeks of beating myself up because I felt that I wasn't accomplishing anything, I wised up and realized that I was actually accomplishing everything that was important at this stage of my life. For a few months, there was only one thing on my checklist, and I learned to be grateful for that blessing and to live in the moment. I realized that my life had changed drastically and that I had to change with it. I redefined "success" and started living in the moment. If the baby was smiling, sleeping, or generally happy, my day was a big success.

The first few months of pregnancy, which generally include nausea, vomiting and sleepless nights, are designed to make parents realize that the days of living for themselves are over and our priorities need to get in line with this new world order. By the time the baby arrives, we are so used to functioning on little sleep that anything over three hours is considered a good night's sleep. After my second child, I was frequently asked whether I was getting enough rest, and my often-surprising reply was, "Yes, I've slept for three hours in a row. I feel rested." Instead of lamenting that I had not left the house in six weeks, I could discuss how nice it was to enjoy my home for a change and just hang out and bond with the baby, and I really meant it. I have an amazing career that I enjoy, but family comes first.

When I had my second son, Giorgio, it was easier to live in the moment. I had no great expectations for my two months of maternity leave. Each day, I limited my goals to two things.

The first was to always have a safe and healthy baby, followed by either a chore to do around the house, or a phone call to make, or a bit of writing to do. If I accomplished anything else, I was Supermom for the day. Adjusting your sail gives you the freedom to live in the moment and to linger and enjoy your current blessings.

SHOULD I LINGER?

I sit by your bed and watch as you fall asleep
I should leave the room now, but I
can't seem to move my feet

There is a noise in the hallway and suddenly you're awake
Joy and anxiety are on the face that I make

I cradle you in my arms, and you caress my nose
It is now your security blanket, not just the star of my pose

Reluctantly, you let go as sleep turns to slumber
Should I have lingered? There is no need to wonder

Island Mindfulness

Mindful living requires practice and dedication to self-awareness. If you are from the islands, the "no problem" mentality may be in your DNA, but change is difficult for everyone, and we all get put to the test. It is a way of thinking and feeling that you have to practice each day. The problems and issues don't go away, but you can change how you react to them.

What is life throwing your way? A new baby, new job, new marriage, loss of a loved one, financial challenges? We can learn something from every situation that we are in. Don't be so quick to get through it that you miss the lesson. And, if possible, try not to suffer through it. So far, you have made it through everything that life has thrown your way, and this will be no different.

> "Be authentically you. The world doesn't revolve around you, but it depends on you. Be consistent. Be your best self. Show up every day like the sunrise, wearing your finest garment, and be ready to shine brightly in every life and every circumstance that you touch."
>
> **JANET AUTHERINE**

Don't Let Anyone Define Who You Are

I was a short, skinny kid. I was not a picky eater, but I had lots of energy, and nothing that I ate would stick to my bones. Friends and family members would tell me, "You are very skinny," and it wasn't in a good way. In my community, skinny was not considered attractive. Girls were supposed to have curves. Although I was generally happy with my appearance, the criticism started to affect my self-esteem, especially in high school. I loved the winter months because that meant that I could wear long pants under my regular clothes, and it would give my body a little shape. Whenever I could, I would wear an extra layer of clothing to appear a little bigger. Finally, in college, I was tired of feeling insecure and made it my mission to gain weight. Since regular meals were not accomplishing my goal, I would supplement meals with Twinkies, candy bars, and Honey Buns. Over the space of about three months, I filled out. I started getting compliments about my new curves. I had no concept of what size was the right size for me because my opinion of myself was based on the opinions of others. I continued living on junk food. Finally, a boyfriend advised me that I was getting a little too round and may want to cut back on the food, and a relative that used to tease me for being too skinny was now commenting that I was getting fat. The thing about putting on weight is that you can't choose where it goes, and the fat was going to my stomach. For the first time, I started feeling legitimately insecure, not because of what others were saying but because I started to feel unhealthy.

I learned from this experience not to let others define me. You can spend a lifetime blowing in the wind if your self-esteem is grounded in the opinions of others because opinions are not facts, and they change often. Your opinion of yourself is the only one that matters. Even our own opinions can and should change because the journey of life is about self-discovery. When someone tells me that I have changed, I take it as a compliment, even though it may not be meant as one and I say, "Thank you; I *have* changed." When someone brags about being the same person that they were in high school, I am skeptical. We change as we get older, gain more life experiences, travel the world, meet new people, and read more books and that change is to be embraced.

SELF-ACTUALIZATION

The moment when everything that you thought was wrong with you becomes an asset.
When you look in the mirror and realize that you

*are perfect just the way that you are.
You struggled because you have been standing
in the wrong room with the wrong people.
Trying to fit in, looking for approval, asking
for permission to be authentically you. That
lightbulb moment usually comes when you
are alone and in quiet meditation. If you are
still searching, find your person, your tribe or
your soulmate. Embrace self-love and acceptance.
Watch the pieces of your mirror come together to
finally reflect all the beauty that is in your heart.
Your moment of self-actualization s the moment
that you finally see your inner beauty; the moment
that you finally believe that you are enough.*

Island Mindfulness

Everyone is not on the same journey, and sometimes you will meet someone who is generally insecure about their own standing in life and who will try to impose their own values, beliefs, and judgments on you. They may sound so confident and self-assured that you start to question your own values and your place in the world. It's always good to listen to someone else's perspective, and if there is a nugget of good advice, take it and ignore the rest. Thank everyone for their opinion and then do what is compatible with the person you are or the person that you are striving to become. Island Mindfulness allows you to listen to your inner voice and let it be your guide.

"We will all have days that are challenging. But we must never give up – strive for excellence, good values, justice, truth and love. People will say all manner of things about you, especially if you have the courage to do things differently, but stand firm."

LISA HANNA

Be the Captain of Your Sailboat

Have you ever found yourself in a situation where you have uttered the following: "God, if you would just get me out of this, I will never…" Against my better judgment, I accepted a ride on a motorcycle because I wanted to be the adventurous girl I am not! During my early years, someone close to me uttered these words, "If you kill yourself doing something dangerous or stupid, I'm not coming to your funeral!" Islanders like to administer doses of tough love. So, if it has any potential of being dangerous, I am not your girl. So, as I was speeding down the highway at 80 miles per hour, holding on for dear life, I uttered the tell-tale words. Thankfully, God wasn't too busy that day and answered my prayer.

Conformist behavior starts in early childhood. Although we are unique beings, at the onset, we naturally imitate the behavior of our parents, and that inclination to follow the leads of those around us can continue well into our adult life. I realized how early peer-pressure starts after enrolling my son in daycare. I think that peer pressure starts at around two years old. On my first visit to the daycare, I was amazed to see all the kids asleep at the same time. I exclaimed that my child would never go for that; he has an independent spirit, and he sleeps when he darn well pleases and not a moment sooner. Boy, was I wrong; within a week he was eating when the other kids ate, playing at a specific time and sleeping on request just like all the other kids. Part of this behavior was the result of a routine, but a large part was early peer pressure; my son observed the other kids eating and wanted to eat; he observed the other kids sleeping and closed his eyes. Every so often, I saw one kid refusing to go along with the crowd. It was frustrating for the daycare provider, but it gave me hope.

When I think about the times in my life that I have gone with the crowd or listened to the opinion of others, most have been insignificant and sometimes even fun—skipping church to go walking through the cane fields in Jamaica or scouting for crabs; sneaking out the house to a party and then staying way too late and having to sneak back in. However, I have also made career decisions that were not in line with my passion and stayed in relationships that were not right for me because of faulty advice. Everyone can be a leader. Take pride in being the leader of your own life. If you are particularly skilled at standing in your own truth, aim to lead others.

Island Mindfulness

We champion uniqueness, individuality, and charting our own course, but it's not easy to be the one standing apart from the crowd. No one wants to be the only one at the rock-and-roll party in a ball gown, but we all have to chart our own course. If you choose to follow the crowd, be mindful of your decision. Know where the crowd is heading and what the consequences are if you follow instead of lead. When everyone is looking to you for an answer, 30 seconds seems like a long time, but take the time to go inward to process the request, hold it up to the light of your moral compass, and make the decision that is right for you. Having meaningful relationships doesn't mean that you have to be the "yes" person in the crowd.

> *"Prejudice is a chain, it can hold you. If you prejudice, you can't move, you keep prejudice for years. Never get nowhere with that."*
>
> **BOB MARLEY**

One Love: Grace in the Face of Prejudices

Jamaica is diverse in its people and culture. Although we are largely of African descent, the motto is "Out of Many One People." We realize that our strength is in our diversity. In my early years, racism was not a part of the daily experience, although "colorism" was sometimes discussed. All my school years prior to college were spent in schools where the students were people of color. The challenges that I faced had to do with my culture—kids aren't always kind to a new kid with a foreign accent. Racism was not discussed in our home, as the focus was on education. Therefore it was not until I enrolled at Penn State University, where the majority of the students were white, that I began to understand the history of racism and the legacy of mental slavery that it left on a generation of people of African descent in the United States and globally.

One morning, while on vacation to the Caribbean, I wrapped up a wonderful breakfast and was heading back to my room with breakfast for my son. As I was walking out of the restaurant, basking in the glow of the Caribbean sun, admiring the beauty of the water, the friendliness of the people, and the tastiness of the food, a fellow tourist interrupted my thoughts by asking me, "Do you work here?" It is the kind of stereotyping that I had come to expect in the US but was surprised to find it on an island soil. He didn't seem to notice that I was seven months pregnant, wearing vacation shades and radiating that happy tourist glow. Grace and the understanding of human nature and our frailties enabled me to smile and tell the gentleman in the restaurant that I was not the waitress and pointed him in the direction of the wait staff. I consciously resisted the temptation to get angry and went back to enjoying the ocean and the summer breeze as I headed back to my room.

I wrote two poems about racial struggle and hope during President Barack Obama's presidency. The first one is about the importance of Dr. Martin Luther King's dream and the second about President Barack Obama, who in many ways was a huge part of that dream realized.

WALKING IN THE FOOTSTEPS OF A KING

Dr. Martin Luther King, Jr. Day is a day to remember that a light that shined on behalf of all humanity was momentarily dimmed in the name of hate but love lit a torch in each of our hearts so that we never forget the sacrifices made, and the paths paved with blood and tears and prayers in order for all of us to live peacefully, as equals.

A day to remember that because of the sacrifices of Dr. King, we can quietly or loudly chant, let freedom ring – for an immigrant child who only hears the sound of doors closing, for a daughter's right to take up space and be safe in her own body, for boys of color to be allowed to exist without fear of the consequences of being feared, and grow up to live the dream that Dr. King envisioned, for every human being to proudly and fearlessly live and walk in their truth.

A day to remember that there can be no silence in the face of injustice that with every resurgence of hate, we can join hearts and hands and harness the power of love to march, legislate, show kindness, open our hearts to the truth that differences are not deficiencies, and create a bigger table that welcomes all our brothers and sisters.

Dr. King taught us that the strength, conviction and action of one person can change the world. Continue to walk in the footsteps of a King. Never stop fighting for the right to live with honor and dignity, as one human race.

BARACK OBAMA

Sandy-haired leader
World on your shoulders
Grayed by power

Emotionally intelligent
Halting speech, biting your tongue
Aiming not to offend but to inform and inspire

Struggling with being the first
Sometimes winning, sometimes losing
Carrying the weight of expectation

Fighting for equality
Fighting pessimism and hate
Fighting for a more perfect union

Multi-cultural light in the dark
Keeping alive the hope that love trumps racial hatred
That love trumps religion differences

You are in our hands
You are in his hands
You are in the hands of history

Keep your head up

Island Mindfulness

We can be mindful of our own journey, but can we take the time to consider the journey of the rest of humanity? The world still struggles with the reality that the same blood runs through our veins and that we are all brothers and sisters. This is particularly true in the United States, where there is still systematic racism, stemming from slavery and Jim Crow laws, and there are still many hateful people who believe that it is justifiable to judge a person by the color of their skin. These prejudices are not innocent; they can and have resulted in death to many people of color. A few years ago, as I was walking to the gym, a teenager drove by me and yelled the "N" word from his pick-up truck. It was shocking and scary but pale in comparison to the loss of Tamir Rice, Trayvon Martin, Philando Castile, and numerous others.

This discussion may feel like it is not your journey, but we are all interconnected; it is important to be mindful of not just your journey but the journey of our brothers and sisters. It is important to make diverse friends, don't make judgments based on the images that we see on television, in movies, on billboards or in books—walk next to someone of a different race and culture and experience their journey. When we are faced with the possibility of making a judgment or a decision that involves someone who seems different from us, it helps to take 30 seconds to examine our perceptions and then the implications for both you and that person if you are wrong. Referring to the president of a company as the assistant because she looks young or because she is a woman, or mistaking a shopper for the salesperson can be remedied by a sincere apology. Calling the police on someone because of the color of their skin makes you fearful and can result in death. These are the times when I appreciate my island upbringing the most. Through that experience, I understand that we are "Out of many, one people." We are all brothers and sisters in love and "one love" is the only love that brings peace to the world.

PART 3:
Mindful Journey To A Purposeful Life

ISLAND MINDFULNESS MANTRA - PURPOSE

I walk in gratitude
I patiently work to discover my purpose and
I am mindful of each moment of the journey
I find meaning in the sun, wing and rain
When rain falls into my life, I embrace my humanity
and never lose sight of the divine

ISLAND MINDFULNESS: HOW TO USE THE TRANSFORMATIONAL
POWER OF MINDFULNESS TO CREATE AN ABUNDANT LIFE
www.janetautherine.com

> "Sun a shine an pot a bwile, but things no bright, bickle no nuff. Rain a fall, river dah flood, but water scarce and dutty tough."
>
> **Ms. Louise Bennett**

Financial Abundance: Rich but Living a Rich and "Irie" Life

Whenever I visit my childhood home back in Jamaica, I marvel at the size of the house that I grew up in. It is a very small two-bedroom flat, which housed three adults and two small children—my brother Mark and I. Both bedrooms combined are the size of my current living room, which I now complain is too small. It had a small kitchen in the center, a tiny room to the left of the kitchen where my mother's brother and cousin lived, and an outhouse at the back of the property. My mama had a reputation for taking in anyone who needed a place to stay, so at any given time, our small piece of paradise had seven to nine occupants. Yet, I didn't feel poor. The house was always meticulously kept, there were fruit trees in the yard, and a Caribbean house wouldn't be complete without flowers in the front—particularly hibiscus plants. The house was filled with love from its occupants, and as a child, I had numerous friends who would stop by throughout the day.

All my friends lived the same way we did. As kids, we would get up early in the morning to go to the town pipe to fetch water and carry it back home because our home like many others, did not have reliable running water. If the local pipe did not have water, we would take the long walk to the river, fill our buckets with water, and carry them on our heads back home. We would then take our baths in a small basin with some of the water that we had brought back to the house, or if we were fortunate that day, we would shower at the outdoor tap and head off to school. These activities were fun, not burdensome, except for the few times when we were having too much fun and spilled our water when we were just a few steps from home.

As kids, going to the market on the weekend was fun. This is where we would buy produce and meat and socialize with our neighbors. Chicken was the meat of choice. However, when funds were low, we settled for "chicken back." Although we knew that we were not rich, we did not feel poor either; however, we did have poor days. It was known in the community that if you were purchasing "chicken back," rather than the prime cuts, such as legs and breasts, your funds were really low.

In Jamaica, most children wore uniforms to school, which served as an equalizer among our peers. Regardless of income, we were all required to wear the same green uniform with a white undershirt. Any parent with a decent iron could afford to send a child off to school looking sharp and feeling good.

Currently, CNN is available in many households in Jamaica, but growing up, we did not have a television in the house (or indoor plumbing or a refrigerator)–those items were symbols of wealth and usually owned by those with great jobs or relatives overseas. As a child, I was always excited to be invited to the homes of such people because we would be offered a nice, cold glass of ice water. Beyond experiencing the luxuries of having ice water or catching a glimpse of a local television program and knowing we didn't have these in our own home, we didn't feel deprived. When I moved to the United States, we lived in a modest apartment in West Philadelphia. My mother was a single parent and worked several jobs to make ends meet. We knew that money was tight, but we didn't feel either poor or hopeless because we were always told that poverty could be solved by getting a good education. It is important that kids have hope. Since education at the primary level was free, we were all on the same playing field, distinguished only by the amount of effort that we were willing to put into our studies.

Island Mindfulness

We can create a rich life without the trappings of the world. Mindfulness and minimalism help us to navigate life with a sense of gratitude, gratitude for being alive, having hope and having the basics for life (food, shelter, and water). Gratitude frees our mind and soul to be exponentially grateful for anything else that we are blessed with. Looking back, a few key factors stand out; I knew that my success or failure was in my own hands; there was no one to blame but myself if I failed, so I had to do well, if for no other reason than for my own pride. It did help that we had limited access to television because we were not constantly bombarded with images of how the other half lived. Regardless of outside forces, we had a sanctuary of safety and love within the household. There was no need to look for love and affinity on the outside, which, unfortunately, is the plight of many of our youths who reach out to gangs to feel like they are a part of a family or succumb to the influence of "bad company" to establish their identities. When I look back and realize how little we survived on without sacrificing happiness, I can say that you are as rich as you feel. When you are surrounded by the love and support of family and friends, it creates a rich and abundant life.

> *"Continuous growth means we are in a constant state of evolution, and it is said that whatever we learn we have an obligation to teach. Our achievements are not ours alone – they also belong to every person who has extended a hand along our journey. Therefore, when we celebrate our accomplishments, we also celebrate those on whose shoulders we stand to allow us to rise. When we lift up others, we lift up ourselves."*
>
> **JANICE P. HOLNESS**

Financial Abundance: Don't Shop with a Hole in Your Basket

After investing many years and making significant financial sacrifices to earn a degree or multiple degrees, there is a strong temptation to show yourself and everyone that it was all worth the time and money by prematurely launching into a lavish lifestyle. My first job in Washington, DC paid a very modest salary. I tried to be responsible by renting a studio apartment, but the rent was $700 a month, plus utilities, groceries, credit card debt and transportation costs. I soon found myself living paycheck to paycheck. Unfortunately, this is typical of most college graduates. Even before students arrive at their dorm rooms, the credit card offers are flooding in. Students start out using them for responsible purchases such as those for books, but before long the cards are used for discretionary items. As soon as we near the credit card limit, miraculously the credit card company offers to increase the spending limit. I didn't have a college fund like some of my classmates, so I survived both college and law school on credit cards. This addictive practice can continue into adulthood with the lure of no-down-payment car loans; purchase now, pay later offers on household items; travel offers from a variety of sources; and interest-only mortgage loans.

When pregnant with my son Giorgio, I started the lengthy process of putting my financial house in order. Faced with having to financially care for a second child, I had no choice but to make responsible decisions. Within a short time, I drafted a will, revocable trust, health-care power of attorney, and purchased life insurance. The truth is that every household needs these basic documents, especially when children are involved, and life insurance is not so expensive if you are a younger individual.

Live below your means. We have all heard stories about individuals working modest wages but leaving a sizable fortune behind; these are the smart savers. They meet and exceed financial wellness goals—the factory worker who left a million dollars to his alma mater, or the next-door neighbor who shopped at discount stores and drove a 10-year-old car but built a local community center or funded their grandchildren's college education. They accomplished this large feat by living below their means and saving. I grew up watching my mother working several jobs and saving as much as she could. She didn't overspend and cherished the things that she worked hard to purchase, and she passed on some valuable lessons—don't buy a new car when the current one runs just fine, take good care of the sofa so it doesn't have to be replaced, eat at home and take good care of clothing so that it lasts for many years. Although I am a very good cook, the advice to eat at home didn't stick; I am a foodie and eating out is one of my not so guilty pleasures.

Although these are simple, almost fool-proof ways of achieving financial wellness, they are difficult to accomplish because of peer pressure—the same peer pressure we faced in kindergarten when our best friend came to school with the new book bag, and you told your parents that you had to get a new one, too. Only now it is the larger house, the latest model car, new golf clubs, the latest PlayStation, or the latest iPhone. We don't need them, but we feel that we deserve them because we have worked hard and should have nice things. Most Americans cannot survive 2 missed paychecks and are making the minimum payment on credit card bills every month; we look good on the outside but if our financial statement was public, the embarrassment would prompt a generational change in how our society views money. It is possible to have an abundant life without wealth but almost impossible if we are not walking in our truth.

Island Mindfulness

In my experience, the road to financial wellness includes, obtaining a solid education, finding a job that rewards your hard work, saving by paying yourself first, starting with that first job, and living below your means (don't be ashamed to downsize for a few years if you need to). If you have an entrepreneurial spirit, don't be afraid to start a business and lay the foundation for generational wealth. It is also essential to create a will, purchase life insurance, and give back through financial contributions to your church and community or to those who are less fortunate. If you are an islander or an immigrant, you are very familiar with sending money back home to relatives and friends. It is culturally significant to honor the tradition of caring for family members back home when you are financially able to do so and helping someone else climb up the ladder.

Today, financial wellness for me means using the lessons learned above to have enough family income to be able to encourage my sons to follow their passion, be it entrepreneurship, art, law, or some other creative pursuit. It means living within my means so that I can leave a legacy for the next generation. Money is not needed to be happy—but not spending the little that you have wisely can certainly lead to unhappiness. If this is not where your strength lies, consider consulting a financial planner. We often bury our heads in the sand when it comes to finances, thinking that maybe if we don't look at our credit score it will be fine, but this is an area where mindfulness is very effective. Be in tune with what things are wants and what things are needs. This is different for everyone. Focus on your needs and never make a hasty decision when purchasing wants. Finally, teach all the financial lessons that you learn on your journey to abundance; when we rise, it is our duty to lift others.

> "When one door is closed, another is open."
>
> **BOB MARLEY**

Include Your Heart when Choosing a Career

I was always the quiet one, the voice of reason, and the peacemaker in my circle. I knew that I wanted a career where I could be of service, but my path was not clear. What was crystal clear was that I would go to college. I attended a vocational technical high school where we learned a trade that could help us in the real world, so college preparation wasn't my main focus. I was immersed in classes that taught me things that would get me an office job—typing and shorthand. However, my typing skills were not stellar, and shorthand was rapidly becoming a dinosaur.

As a struggling immigrant, financial stability played a significant role in my career choice. When your parents work hard to create opportunities, you want to grab every opportunity so that you can be successful. I didn't have dreams of becoming wealthy, just of having enough money to buy a house, pay the bills and, like most immigrants, maybe send a few dollars back home. Naturally, when I had the opportunity to choose a major, I chose business. I didn't have a passion for business, but it conjured up thoughts of a solid, secure future.

The thing about not having a passion for whatever you are doing is that you tend not to do it well, and I eventually changed my major to labor and industrial relations because of my strong interest in resolving disputes. The downside about choosing a path that you love is that sometimes it does not pay well. When I graduated, a labor and industrial relations degree was not very attractive to employers, so the next logical step was law school. My choice to pursue law school surprised many of my friends and family because they couldn't imagine someone as introverted as me becoming an attorney. I had very little interest in litigating but was passionate about dispute resolution. The practice of law is a career choice that I knew could provide a balance between my desire to provide service to the community and financial success.

Island Mindfulness

What will motivate you to bounce out of bed every day and go to work? I often hear people declare that "I am not my job." That may be true, but your job is where you will spend the majority of your waking hours; it is surprising how much of an impact it has on your health and happiness. So, let your heart be your guide when choosing a career. It may not be possible for your first job to be what your heart desires, but always be mindful of where you are and of the path you need to take to get to your dream job. Don't be surprised when doors that you really want to enter close; if it is the door that is meant for you, it will open when you are prepared to enter. You may even have to kick in some doors or climb through a window.

Keep in mind that you may find your purpose only to discover that the path is a long and winding one. In my late 30s, I found my happy place professionally as an administrative law judge, which allowed me to serve, listen, and resolve disputes. I also started writing more poetry and blogging about my life in my Growing into Greatness blog. But I have also worked as a salesperson in a department store, in a job processing mail at the post office (in which we had to ask for permission to go to the bathroom), as an administrative assistant (AFTER obtaining my law degree), as a tax/administrative attorney (which was a great job, but introverts usually don't function well when attending constant meetings), and in numerous other jobs before I finally found a career that is compatible with my personality and purpose. In each job, I rose above the frustrations and excelled. Seeing my mother work jobs that she didn't always love, taught me the value of hard work and dedication to one's duty. Not having what you consider to be your dream job is not an excuse to give up on pursuing excellence. The universe is ready to support your journey once to start down the path to your purpose. Being mindful of your professional journey requires taking the time to reflect on where you are on the path and decide if you should continue to change course.

> "God sent me on Earth. He sends me to do something, and nobody can stop me. If God wants to stop me, then I stop. Man never can."
>
> **BOB MARLEY**

Strengths & Weaknesses: The Doctor Bird Flies Backwards & the Parrot Speaks

Many years ago, I watched an enlightening interview on 60 Minutes. The expert discussed how students who are great in English but poor in math spend so much time trying to improve their math scores that they don't capitalize on their natural strength to master language arts or another subject. He posed the question: if your child had a C in math and an A in English, which one would you focus on? Almost universally, the answer was the C in math. Of course, there is nothing wrong with trying to improve that C to a B, it's just that so many parents try to get the C to an A, that they don't realize that maybe the child has a natural gift for the English language and that is where the primary time and resources should be spent. The same thing occurs in the workplace; we often don't play to the strengths of each team member. We hit the holy grail of productivity and innovation when each team member is doing what they love and what comes naturally to them.

Wouldn't it be revolutionary if we were all able to identify our strengths, our gifts, our purpose and spend our time nourishing, developing, executing, living that purpose-driven life? For some, that would make for a very boring life because personal and professional growth flows from the self-discovery and the struggle. As an introvert, I have always enjoyed operating in my comfort zone. Since kindergarten, my "negative" comment has been, "Janet is so quiet." "I wish she would speak up more." And, by the way, she is also a hard worker, she writes well and is well-behaved in class. For years, I struggled to come out of my shell the way most of the authorities in my life wanted me to, but when I did, it didn't feel authentic. I lived with that insecurity until one day when I read the book *The Introvert Advantage*, and the lightbulb went off—I am an introvert. I speak when I have something important to say, and I will be darned if I am going to yap just for the hell of it to show that I know more or as much as other people or to appease those who are uncomfortable with silence. I identified my skills (listening, writing, problem resolution) and was blessed to find a job that allowed me to maximize those skills, instead of sitting in meetings all day with that uncomfortable feeling that I should say more. Oh, the wonderful power of a book. Books can transform lives by allowing us to learn more about ourselves. My heroes are the great writers, such as Maya Angelou and Marti Olsen Laney who wrote *The Introvert Advantage* and changed the course of my life.

Island Mindfulness

What comes naturally to you? We all have natural and unique gifts. Identify what they are and focus on developing in those areas that you are your most authentic self. If you are afraid of danger, why take a job as a firefighter or a policewoman? If you hate numbers, why study tax or accounting? If you have always loved teaching kids, take that job as a teacher, not as an administrator or a principal just because it pays more. You will be managing teachers, doing paperwork but spending less time with kids unless they are sent to the principal's office.

There are times that we have to operate outside our comfort zone, but you should at least be mindful of why you are doing so and give yourself a deadline to get back to the thing that makes you excited to go to work each day and what makes you grateful to be alive. I am a big fan of taking chances and trying new things—but it's best to just visit places outside your comfort zone—if you like the place or experience then stay, if not, don't buy property there. When I reflect on career or major life choices, it reminds me of traveling to many beautiful islands but only feeling at home in a few. Choose home.

> "Don't worry about a thing; every little thing is gonna be alright."
>
> **BOB MARLEY**

Island Time: There is Joy in Being Patient

"Island Time" is a way of living; it is the humorous way to describe island mindfulness. It is embracing the moment for as long as it takes to fully absorb the experience. When I lived in Jamaica, my mama would take us to the bank in Morant Bay most Saturday mornings to deposit a few dollars and to check to see if we had earned any interest on our small savings account. Even a few cents in interest was cause for excitement. There was no rush. We were not in and out in 10 minutes; it usually took over an hour and sometimes several hours of waiting before we made it to the window. This was so normal that I didn't give it a second thought. Many years later, I tried banking in Jamaica, and while the wait wasn't as long as when I was a child, it created impatience and anxiety. I had become Americanized, and Americans don't usually operate on "island time." We are a "just do it, get it, achieve it, and do so right now" society.

There are times when impatience is needed, but I love the island time mentality. It is slowing down to be mindful of every moment. To chat with neighbors, to not rush every activity, to not be so busy that life is something that just happens to us. The trip to the bank was not just about getting money; it was a chance to catch up with friends and family and find out how their week went, how their children were doing, and if they had any struggles or achievements that week. It is how we learned if there were any celebrations happening or a funeral (funeral watch nights had music, dancing, good food, and drinks to celebrate the life of the dearly departed). There was no rush because no one was interested in rushing. This was the community center. We saw many of the same neighbors every week. The same is true for dining at many restaurants, especially the ones outside of the tourist areas; they are places to have a leisurely meal while catching up with friends. Don't expect the service to be fast, (and complaining won't help).

My greatest test of patience came when I was 12. My brothers and I were awaiting our visas so we could join our mother in the United States. We each received an envelope containing our interview dates with the immigration service. We opened two of the letters, and after noticing that the dates were the same, we assumed that the dates were the same for all three. They were not. I missed my appointment date and had to wait another year for a new date. My brothers went to the US more than a year earlier than I did. To an 11-year-old, it was devastating, and the extra year of waiting felt like 10 years. However, while I impatiently waited, I started a new school, made new friends, and learned that mishaps happen and that we can survive them with grace. I learned that your purpose is not just a destination, it is a journey and the journey can be quite unpredictable and thrilling.

Island Mindfulness

That experience also taught me that waiting doesn't have to be passive; it can be very active. You can accomplish many things that are important to you while in waiting mode. Waiting does not mean moping around and complaining. It means that you have time to mentally prepare for what's next. You need to be ready when your opportunity arrives. Although I would rather not spend a few hours in the bank, what I wouldn't give for a 2-hour siesta every day to have a leisurely lunch, browse a bookstore, take a nap, or just write. My exercise in patience is to meditate for up to 30 minutes each morning. It requires discipline and mental focus, sometimes the mind is blank, and sometimes, I am looking for answers that never come. In our fast-paced world, it is hard to just BE, but we have to try.

> "A lot of legends, a lot of people, have come before me. But this is my time."
>
> **USAIN BOLT**

Procrastination or Mindful Delay

I sometimes develop the urge to cook dinner, clean the apartment, organize my bookshelf, or organize the sock drawer. This usually means that I have an exam or a writing deadline, and so I need to procrastinate. All these things are important but not as urgent as the task at hand.

I started outlining this book in 2006, and it's being published in 2020! There have been years in which I did not write a single word. It would be easy to put a positive spin on it and say that I was busy birthing three children and just wasn't ready to birth a book, but procrastination played a large role in the delay. I kept telling myself that with kids and a full-time job, I didn't have the time to write, but I did. It just didn't make it to the top five things on my priority list. The most important part of being a writer is to write. The key to becoming a successful writer is to write consistently. Writing every day is possible...15 minutes in the morning, half an hour at lunch, an hour after the kids go to bed, a few minutes before everyone else in the house wakes up. It's not about time; it's about priorities.

I used to say that I procrastinated because I work better under pressure, but sometimes procrastination is born out of fear. Fear of undertaking something, fear of completing something, fear of failure, fear of success. When it is your time, don't be hampered by fear, and don't let the spirit of procrastination keep you from achieving the dreams that can only work if you do.

WHILE WE WAIT

While we wait for our calling, our job is to be useful
Let us build a mansion with pearly gates and
streets paved with gold in the depths of our hearts
to welcome in saints and sinners,
the beaten and the downtrodden, the lost and the broken
We are all human beings. Same destination
but a different journey.

We will pool our tears and conspire to live life on Earth
boldly, freely, joyfully, lovingly, peacefully
Alone, each teardrop falls painfully to the ground
Together, we have the resilience of the ocean

Island Mindfulness

The world depends on us to be useful. Take a breath and ask yourself why you are delaying taking action. Realistically, when does it need to get done? What are the steps that need to be taken to make progress and what is a reasonable timeline? Don't set yourself up for failure by building unreasonable expectations. Finally, determine how you can carve out time in your day to accomplish your goals.

Sometimes, the time just isn't right, or the project isn't ripe for completion; if so, then move it down your list of things to accomplish and stop stressing about it. This is a mindful delay. It will free up your mind to handle your more urgent tasks. When I started outlining this book in 2006, I was 36, parenting one child and thought that I was too busy. Now, I am a single parent of three very active boys. Busy has taken on a new meaning, but it shows that being busy is relative; no matter how busy you are, you can always find the time for what is really important. Priorities change quickly, so focus on your top three most important things to accomplish each week and the most important thing to accomplish each day because life happens, and our goals can instantly change. Most importantly, be mindful of what your heart, mind, and soul need for you to be both physically and mentally healthy enough to do your best work and be your best self.

> "I've got to pick myself up, dust myself
> off and start all over again."
>
> **PETER TOSH**

Death and Divorce: Rough Sea but Able Captain

My brother was stationed in Hawaii, so I had the pleasure of visiting the island a few times. On a trip to Maui, I witnessed many fearless people on horseback climbing the mountains; they were able to put their trust in an animal when two missteps either to the right or left could send you over a cliff. They didn't live in fear of the unexpected and it dawned on me that you need to be up high to see many of the beautiful things in this world. Still, I'd rather you take me on a rollercoaster that is fast but with only a few tiny drops and nothing that could produce a heart attack. Take me on a boat ride with beautiful views of nature and the ocean. I don't mind some rough waves in our path. I prefer when there is constant movement in life but when nothing really bad is happening, and nothing great is really happening either; we are just coasting along watching the moving sand. I have to admit that I like coasting along. I am usually a bit uncomfortable with emotional highs, and I dislike emotional lows. Whenever something wonderful happens, I sometimes wonder if something bad will also happen—it is the yin and yang of life. But, growing up in a Jamaican household, I've learned to expect that challenges are a normal part of life. You don't go looking for trouble, especially when it involves minding someone else's business, but you focus on the problem and handle it responsibly when it comes along.

My friends who know me well used to refer to me as Dr. Spock because I project an image of calm and self-assuredness, and in most situations, I tend to downplay the emotion and focus on just the facts and the practical solution. I am not prone to emotional highs and lows, with the exception of love and a few emotionally complex pregnancies. As an introvert, most of my conflicts tend to occur quietly and internally. My emotional highs are few and memorable—joining my family in the United States, graduations, especially from law school, the birth of my children, every time that I have fallen in love, getting my dream job as an administrative law judge, finishing the Marine Corps Marathon, President Obama's victory, and a few other notables.

The lows have also been memorable—the death of my Mama Linett, who raised me until age 12, the death of many of her relatives who I grew up with, a broken engagement, a divorce, and the struggles of single parenthood, not finding a job immediately after law school, the loss of an important friendship, the young adult struggles to fit in and find my purpose and some persistent health issues (thyroid and fibroids) that required surgeries. I have discussed some of these struggles throughout this book, but two stand out—divorce and death. First, through most of Mama Linett's final years, I was still studying and trying to establish a career.

She died before I was able to provide her with more financial assistance. She also wanted to see me happily married with children but passed away before I had my beautiful boys. She would have been so proud of them, and they would have brought her immense joy. However, I am living the life that she would want for me, and I make sure that her grandchildren know her story.

Second, I grew up in a single-parent household (both in Jamaica and in Philadelphia), and although I had a friendly relationship with my father, it wasn't the close father/daughter bond that I wanted. Most of my childhood, he lived in Toronto while I was in Philadelphia. My wish for myself was to get married and stay married and create what society deems to be an ideal family life for my children. I waited to get married until I was a mature 30, many of my professional goals were established, and I was ready to focus on family. The marriage lasted 13 years and died over a six-year period after many years of counseling to resolve fundamental differences. Divorce is death; the death of dreams, goals, promises, a way of life, parts of the soul, and the human spirit. It also felt like failure. We are taught that if you just put in the work, things will work out and sometimes that does not happen. I have spent most of my life both personal and professional as a listener, mediator, and problem-solver, but I encountered problems that, despite my best efforts, were beyond my ability to solve.

Through meditation, prayer, and the study of human nature, I learned that not every ending is a failure; it is just the conclusion of one part of your journey. Sometimes, God places people in our lives for a fleeting time to accompany us on a particular part of our journey, to teach us lessons or for us to teach them lessons. Taking vows doesn't always change that trajectory. We lose them by death, divorce, or other unforeseen circumstances. Recovery takes an understanding of human nature, acceptance, and the ability to create new dreams and a new life that is still in line with your purpose though perhaps, in unexpected ways. The legacy of divorce is usually children who are counting on us to be our best selves even in the most challenging of circumstances. In my case, I have three beautiful boys who are relying on me to be an able captain even in rough seas.

SETBACKS

are an opportunity to
Slow down
Evaluate your life goals
Take time to change direction
Break barriers
Accept assistance in order to accelerate growth
Calm any fears
Steadfastly continue to grow into your greatness

Island Mindfulness

So, you are boldly walking into your purpose and you trip over a fallen tree that you would have noticed if you were mindful. Or you walked confidently through a glass door that shattered all around you and you are embarrassed and shell-shocked. Or on a beautiful morning jog, a bear appears in your path and your life hangs in the balance. Plan with the awareness that everything can change. Mindfulness helps us lean into that change with the realization that we plant many seeds in life; some die and some flourish. I have learned that good times don't last forever, and bad times don't last forever. That perspective is most useful during the down times; knowing that if you hang in there long enough, your situation will change and the pain will go away and you will be able to feel joy again – is a source of enormous strength through the cycle of life. Have you ever lost a first-love and thought that your world was ending and that you would never love like that again, and two years later you were in love again, and it felt wonderful? Have you wondered how someone who has lost a parent or child can ever recover? We are resilient beyond measure. Each moment passes so quickly that we can't be mindful of them all, but we can try to be aware of our current state of being. So, when the bad times come, there is no need to run from the emotions, no need to drink or smoke them away, take a pill or engage in any self-destructive behavior. Experience the emotion, get counseling if needed, try to figure out if there is a lesson to be learned, and know that good times are just over the bend, and if you are at the bottom of the bell, then the top is the only place left to go. It is a brief stop on the journey; the world continues to turn.

> "The greatness of a man is not in how much wealth he acquires, but in his integrity and his ability to affect those around him positively."
>
> **BOB MARLEY**

Footprints in the Sand of Life

Do we leave our own footprints in the sand or do we spend most of our lives living out a purpose that has already been pre-destined for us? I used to love to watch the movie Sliding Doors because I was intrigued by the concept of divine intervention vs. happenstance. In the movie, actress Gwyneth Paltrow is shown leading two separate lives, almost as if in an alternate universe. It all stemmed from one small decision—whether or not to run for a train. In one life, she misses the train and gets home to a happy boyfriend; in her other life, she runs for and catches the train and also catches her boyfriend having an affair. In real life, there are many similar stories—a man was running late for the office and wasn't in the building when the tragedy of 9/11 occurred, or a woman switched seats on her flight, and it helped her to survive when her airplane crashed. Are these occurrences coincidence or divine intervention? It is ok to be curious and to ask challenging questions. Don't worry that someone is questioning your sanity or your faith.

It is possible that certain aspects of our lives are planned—our birth, our death, those we were meant to encounter along the way, and we only get to color in the blank spaces—but the structure is already outlined for us. The universe is vast, and our knowledge is limited, so I leave room for greater awareness and understanding. However, what I know for sure is that we are all here to live a purposeful life and to accomplish one or many great things. When we think of accomplishing great things, we generally think of rising to the presidency of the United States, winning the Nobel Prize, or becoming a well-known actress. However, fame and fortune are not always the best indicators of success. Service to others should be valued just as highly. We get to choose what footprints we want to leave in the sand. It is ok if our goal changes as we grow. In my 20s, I was chasing a law degree; in my early 30s, my goal was to start a family and have a respectable title at work. I measured my success by what type of friend, spouse, and mother I had become and whether I was achieving balance in my life. Now, I measure success by whether I am raising healthy, happy, well-rounded children. Good friends, a happy family, service to the community, and sharing bits of inspiration through writing are the footprints that I am aiming to leave in the sand.

Island Mindfulness

Whether it is happenstance or even divine intervention, what we do with our time on this earth matters. It matters that we do our best to leave positive footprints in the sand. A few years ago, I started a blog—Women Leaving Footprints in the Sand to tell the untold stories of women who are serving their communities with grace. More of these stories need to be told so that we can learn from each other and so that all the wonderful people who shape our world are recognized in some small way.

Even if the outlines of our lives have already been drawn, there is a lot of room to fill it in with a variety of amazing colors. We can create a rich and colorful life by identifying our purpose, through careful planning, hard work, pursuing our dreams and goals, and following our hearts when it is pulling us. Rise above every obstacle in your way and have the inner strength to hold steadfast to your ideals and dreams.

Mindfulness is refusing to let life just happen to you without your full awareness and active participation. Island mindfulness is being aware that you are a small but significant voice in the world. Although you may be surrounded by water (literally or figuratively), your mind has the ability to relax in the present moment and live harmoniously with all the earth, sun, wind, and rain that will touch your life. By focusing on mindful living and being, the mind, heart, and soul can be Irie (at peace).

PART 4:

Mindful Journey To Spiritual Abundance

ISLAND MINDFULNESS MANTRA
-CONSCIOUSNESS

This is my moment, my journey
I chose mindful living and being as my path
I am present for every step of the journey
I embrace Island Mindfulness so that my mind
and soul are at peace and in my heart, Everything is Irie

ISLAND MINDFULNESS: HOW TO USE THE TRANSFORMATIONAL
POWER OF MINDFULNESS TO CREATE AN ABUNDANT LIFE

www.janetautherine.com

"Self discovery is just as important as self preservation. I have seen how many people earnestly search for a myriad of things in life; similarly, I have seen many found different things. They last only temporarily, only after intense reflection, I realized that I have a simple advice for myself and others: find yourself and keep it."

ODENE M JAMES

Flying High – Keep Your Mind Centered on Truth, Not Fear

We are all connected to the universe; spiritual abundance comes from knowing your connection point so that it can serve as an anchor for you in challenging times. My anchor has been my faith in God. When I wrote this chapter, I was somewhere over the Caribbean ocean. The captain had turned on the seatbelt sign, signaling turbulence was to come, and I was quickly reminded of how much I disliked flying. I always feel like I'm a sitting duck when I'm in the air, so I was distracting myself by writing. When you fly, it is one of the few times in life when you completely turn over control of your life to someone else. I am usually not reassured by the instructions of the able crew. In a true emergency, will the oxygen mask truly fall from its compartment? In a panic, will I remember that the exit row is four rows behind me and to grab my seat cushion to use as a floatation device? The truth is—although well-documented research and common sense tell me that flying is the safest method of travel, I still get a sinking feeling in my heart and stomach every time the airplane hits a bump in the sky. I know that I am not alone. The fear of flying, trips to the dentist, and public speaking are all everyday realities that haunt us.

I boarded an airplane for the first time in 1982 when I emigrated from Jamaica. Although I was nervous about what life would be like at the other end of the ocean, I don't remember ever thinking that I might not get there. I could look out the window of the airplane and enjoy the view. I could not pinpoint when actual fear set in and set out to claim a place in my consciousness. I have always been a cautious but highly optimistic person. No doubt, we all experience this at some level; for some of us, it is flying or sailing, and some have even compared public speaking to losing control and placing yourself at the mercy of the audience.

Island Mindfulness

So how do we handle this feeling that we are powerless? First, we acknowledge that this is a common human experience. We have all felt a loss of power or control in some regard; maybe we are in a relationship in which we have given up our power to someone else, a job that we feel bound to because our financial security depends on it, or a political stand that we have taken for which the fear of being labeled a flip-flopper now prevents us from experiencing and acknowledging personal growth. Second, we picture the end result that we desire; for me, it is landing safely. Third, we call on whatever or whomever we rely on for our source of strength in vulnerable times. For some of us, it is research—there is a 99.9% chance that this plane will land safely. For others it is spiritual—I am in God's hands and although I feel powerless at this moment, He will see me through. For others, it is meditation or positive affirmation—I may not feel in control at this point in my life, but I am in control of my own destiny, and if I can just focus on the result that I desire, I can achieve it. Some of us are fortunate enough to be able to draw on history—I have flown many times before, and even with a lot of turbulence, I landed safely.

Six hours later, as I sat on a balcony overlooking the ocean, I was totally at peace. I looked out at the vastness of the sea, watched the waves as they hit the shoreline, enjoyed the beauty and strength of the coconut trees, and saw endless possibilities. I am not sure if I was any more in control of my destiny than I had been on that airplane, but it sure felt that way. I think the difference is that, both mentally and physically, my feet were firmly planted on the ground.

> *"My dream is to live a good life and be loving, be close to God and be a good human being and bring peace to people."*
>
> **Ziggy Marley**

Connected Hearts and Hands

We all like to think of ourselves as being independent, self-reliant, and able to navigate this world alone. However, rarely is anything accomplished alone. Most of us enter this world surrounded by doctors and nurses, family members, and the mother who carried us for up to nine months. Our connection to and reliance on family and strangers continues throughout our entire lives. As we grow, we rely on the wisdom and knowledge of our teachers and mentors. We rely on friends for emotional support; we rely on our significant other for love and a sense of security. Every day, we rely on complete strangers to safely operate the train we take to work, to maintain the elevators that we take to our dorm rooms, and to protect our children during the school day. Thinking that we are not reliant on others divides us and gives a false sense of superiority. My heart breaks when I see children in poverty, knowing that children do not determine the time, place, or economic circumstances of their birth; they just try to exist in or rise above their circumstances. Whether you are a middle-class

American, a family living in fear and poverty in a war-torn nation, or the wealthy heir to the British throne, the same blood runs through our veins.

A few years ago, I was returning by train from a business trip to New York. I was standing at the train station, which can be a little intimidating if you are not a New Yorker, and an older homeless lady asked me for some money. I reached into my wallet and handed her a $5 bill. She grabbed my hand, thanked me profusely, and began to pray for me. I got caught up in the moment and closed my eyes for a minute. I then realized that I was in a strange place with a stranger and pulled away slightly. I thanked the woman for the prayer and walked away, but I felt changed by the experience. This older stranger reminded me of the healing and praying hands of all the elderly women that I encountered in church and at home. Their prayers were powerful. We are all connected; we just have to look beyond each other's outer appearance and socioeconomic status and open our hearts and minds to the humanity in our brothers and sisters.

ORGANIC CONNECTION IS LIFE-AFFIRMING

Human connectedness isn't only through technology
We are wired together through our
smiles, tears, love, and fears
Our organic need for food, water, and shelter
Our life-affirming desire for peace
Our strength is in these common bonds that keep
us connected throughout the universe
Our consciousness of our organic connectedness

is essential to our love and acceptance of each other and to the survival of humanity.

Island Mindfulness

Reflect on our shared journey. We are connected to our family, friends, and complete strangers in parts of the world that we have never visited. We laugh, we cry, we are prone to similar illnesses, and all our bodies are fragile. We all need a shoulder to lean on. The more we realize our similarities and lend a helping hand to each other, the stronger we become individually and as a society. What we feel in our hearts affects how we lend a helping hand. Thinking of people as "other" or "them" immediately creates a mental divide that allows us to carry on with our lives and ignore the inequities in our society. Choose a cause that is close to your heart —failing schools, overcrowded prisons, the plight of immigrants, our polluted environment...and dive in. Whenever I am going through a rough patch and I find it difficult to pray or meditate, I ask myself how I can be of assistance to someone else. It is a win-win. It takes the focus off my current troubles and instead of feeling helpless or vulnerable, I feel helpful and empowered. Peace starts with hands and hearts that are connected in love.

> "Life can be unforgiving when distributing pain. When you hurt, help; the more you hurt, the more your help. Pain starts to die when love walks in."
>
> **JANET AUTHERINE**

Emotional Fortitude: Strength of the Lignum Vitae

Many years ago, I was in a relationship that started out well but that deteriorated. I would try to end the relationship, but the separation was always short-lived. In hindsight, there were no physical strings keeping me attached; I could have just walked away. However, the younger you are, the more susceptible you are to emotional blackmail. After months of pain and guilt, I still couldn't determine how to exit without causing harm, so I resorted to what my mama taught me: I prayed my way out of it. One day, I cautiously said, "Maybe someone out there would be better for you." For the first time, he didn't protest. I didn't wait for him to change his mind. I hugged him goodbye and didn't look back.

In a time of need, where do you find your emotional strength? I was on the beautiful island of Aruba, celebrating my friend Jackie's birthday, enjoying the pristine beaches and the natural beauty of the cactus (my only worry was the iguana under my breakfast table but I was being strong) when I got a call that my kids had been in a car accident. It is frightening when a phone call starts with, "Are you sitting down?" Aruba is an island that already puts you in the mood to meditate, practice yoga, and pray, so I immediately prayed.

What is your source of strength? Having grown up in the church, I rely on God for emotional strength and support. If I am happy, I say thanks; if I am sad, I pray for strength; if I am feeling discouraged, I pray for inspiration; if I need money, a job, or a friend, I pray for it. As I have gotten older, my view of God has expanded. However, I still believe that there is a God, and when I pray for something, I expect that my prayers will be answered because this is what has happened in most cases. It may not be answered immediately, and the answer may not take the exact form of the request, but it is almost always answered. Often, the answer is not the one that we want to hear but is exactly what we need. I have prayed for a certain job, and God said, "Are you sure that you want that job? Maybe what you really want is a job that makes you feel that you are contributing to society. That job is not ready yet; give me another six months." We all need a source of strength.

Many of my friends are not grounded in faith but are kind and loving with beautiful hearts. They find refuge in meditation, counseling services, the support of sisters/friends, the wisdom of their elders (my grandmother was very wise, and I still remember her advice), self-confidence (I tell myself that "I am a strong, wonderful person, deserving of love and success") and throwing themselves into charity work.

Island Mindfulness

We all need a source of strength to sustain us through the ups and downs of life. I find inner strength to be the most reliable source of strength; anything artificial is temporary and is like stepping into quicksand.

Think about what has sustained you in the past, if it is destructive, search for another source of strength. If you can't come up with anything on your own, read about the experiences of survivors. Seek advice from friends and family members who you trust. I bet they have inspiring stories of love, loss, and surviving difficult times. Don't be too proud to seek the help of a counselor. The beauty of mindfulness is that it allows you to be fully connected and promotes peace from within.

> *"Clear all the self-defeating clutter from your mind and return to love; it is the only word that the universe wrote next to your name."*
>
> **JANET AUTHERINE**

Let the Universe Guide your Journey

My visits to Jamaica bring me back to me; maybe it is the island breeze or the spirit of my answers that are present. My visits brings me back to Debbie, the little girl who skipped on the way to school, digged yam for dinner, carried water on her head, climbed trees to pick fruits and fell out of the tree when she encountered a lizard, falling in a mix of terror and laughter. My inner free-spirit is often lost in the hustle and bustle of daily life. I became quite goal-oriented when I moved to the United States; I wanted to do well in school, achieve success and make my friends and family proud because I was fortunate to have been given an opportunity that I didn't want to waste. I almost always had a list that I proudly checked off daily; that feeling of accomplishment kept me warm. However, in my 40s, my inner free spirit re-emerged. I felt confident enough in the person that I was at that moment to leave a few boxes unchecked. I started learning to celebrate who I was in that moment; not yesterday or tomorrow.

I have taken more wonderful girl's trip that I ever imagined but a few years ago, I decided to take a solo trip just to write. I ran into some friends at the airport and spent a few hours with them; that happens when you are from Jamaica and going to Jamaica for a hideaway. I checked into the Jamaica Inn in an amazing room overlooking the sea and my plan was just to write, no leaving the resort, no distractions. One afternoon when I was sitting on the beach, one of the owners of the Jamaica Inn approached me to chat and I shared that I was writing a book about my journey to mindfulness. I learned that he also practices mindfulness so I paused my writing and just listened to his journey. The universe just presented me with a gift – a gift of knowledge so I had to stop writing what I currently know and be open to learning something new. He gifted me the book, Self Observation by Red Hawk, which opened my mind to a side of consciousness that I was unaware of. There are no coincidences; sometimes, the universe will guide your path if you create room for it.

Island Mindfulness

Sometimes mindfulness is just looking in the mirror and asking, who am I in this moment and am I living the life of abundance that I desire? Put down the checklist and tap into how your mind, body and spirit connects to the rest of humanity. Focus on the beauty that is in you right now. Island mindfulness allows you to remember the person that you were before you cared so much about the opinion of others, when you could feel freedom in your bones. There is no need to live in the past but we cannot ignore our roots. Give the universe permission to act on your behalf. Allow yourself to blow in the wind for a time and see where it takes you. Yes, keeping paying your bills and refrain for doing anything that will cause harm to yourself and others but for everything else, pray, meditate, free the mind and let the universe be your guide.

> "When you understand your inner self –
> your passions, motivations, moral code and
> vulnerabilities, you don't have to blow in
> the wind of someone else's expectations;
> you can stand firm in your own truth."
>
> **JANET AUTHERINE**

Legal and Moral Judgments: Enjoy the Sand but Avoid the Sinkholes

If I go to the beach and see a sign that says, "High Tide No Swimming," I am not swimming. That was my experience on a recent trip to the beach. A few of us were so cautious that we camped out far away from the shoreline because we didn't want to get wet when the waves approached. Others didn't swim but stayed at the edge of the water and enjoyed getting their toes wet. Quite a few completely ignored the sign and were having a blast swimming. Are they reckless, strong swimmers, or did they just not see the sign? When you haven't walked in someone's shoes, you don't know what life experiences inform their decision-making. As such, it is good to operate in the "no judgment" zone for decisions as simple as whether swimming is appropriate to those as complex as decisions involving faith. In this book, I am sharing my thoughts and beliefs based on the path that I have traveled but respect differing perspectives based on the journey of each reader.

My walk has been guided by my experience during my formative years at Hampton Court Seventh Day Adventist Church in Jamaica. The Ten Commandments were our principal guide. Most of us are familiar with them, but they are:

1. Thou shalt have no other gods before me.
2. Thou shalt not make unto thee any graven image.
3. Thou shalt not take the name of the Lord thy God in vain.
4. Remember the Sabbath day, to keep it holy.
5. Honor thy father and thy mother.
6. Thou shalt not kill.
7. Thou shalt not commit adultery.
8. Thou shalt not steal.
9. Thou shalt not bear false witness against thy neighbor.
10. Thou shalt not covet… anything that is thy neighbor's.

My faith has evolved from a mostly rules-based faith to one focused on love and service: "Love God with all thy heart… love thy neighbor as thyself. On these two commandments hang all the law and the prophet." John 3:16. This has significant meaning to me and is a daily reminder to treat everyone with love, respect, and kindness. For my young readers who are dealing with peer pressure on a daily basis and who are often making decisions in the "grey" areas of life, I offer some additional thoughts based on my personal journey.

Honor your mother and father. This is a universal island value. Our parents care for us, and we care for them. You will find several generations living in the same home because, in both the good times and when illness and old age occur, we stick together and care for each other. As a parent, this may be my new favorite commandment. This is particularly tough during your teenage years when parents seem to know very little and communicating with them is almost impossible. In your early 20s, you begin to realize that they are not so bad and start to see them as individuals with good and bad characteristics, rather than just parents. I am not sure if you'd ever love your parents as much as when you begin to have your own children; a new baby's sleepless nights help you find new respect for your parents' dedication, your children's terrible two's make you wonder how your parents ever survived. And when your parents turn into "grandparents," you wonder who these people are, and whether they were ever this kind and loving to you; of course, you are too grateful to complain. I recently read Michelle Obama's book, Becoming and I was moved by her close relationship with the parents and her appreciation for her extended family. She moved back in with her parents after law school and that time with her parents—especially her dad who suffered from MS—was priceless.

Do not covet. I think of this one as "Stop trying to keep up with the Joneses." It's great to have dreams and aspirations, but work at your own pace, and don't worry that your friend finished college before you, or got married and had a baby before you, bought a new car and a new house, or is spending the summer backpacking in Europe. Walk or run at your own pace; you will reach your destination at just the right time. I attended a vocational high school, which prepared students for either college or the workforce. Many of my friends went into the workforce, and shortly after graduation, they were buying new cars and taking fantastic vacations. In the meantime, I was surviving on student loans and spending my summers working at the post office for minimum wage. I didn't doubt that I was on the right train; I just wanted it to get to its destination quicker.

Do not steal. That free cable that the cable company forgot to turn off when the last tenant moved out of your apartment. Is this an extra blessing from heaven or is it stealing? You hand the Starbucks clerk $10 to buy a $3 latte, and she hands you $17 in change. She doesn't notice, and the next customer is impatiently waiting for you to move on, you have 3 seconds to decide if you should hand her back the extra $10. Most of the decisions that test our moral footing are made when no one is watching—meaning we are our own judge and jury. You are your own arbiter of truth and every decision or compromise has the potential of chipping away at your soul.

Do not bear false witness. We should speak the truth at all times, but we don't always, sometimes for reasons that society accepts. Studies show that we tell what we consider to be small untruths several times per day. If someone asks, "How are you?" your automatic response is, "Fine, thanks." Well, you just got laid off from your job, and the rent and tuition payments are due, your boyfriend just broke up with you by text message, and you are barely holding back the tears. Someone says, "Nice day we are having," and you respond, "Yes," but you think, "Are you kidding me?" "An Eskimo couldn't survive in this weather!" These are what we can call "comfortable" lies. You actually feel good about yourself for telling them. The problem with "comfortable" lies is that they make it so much easier to tell the bigger ones.

Refrain from gossiping or sharing information that will cause harm to others. Don't lose sight of what your truth is but recognize that it is a big world and some truths are based on life experiences—so judge others kindly if their perspective is different from yours.

Love thy neighbor as thyself. If you suffer from low self-esteem, this one is either very easy because you always treat everyone better than your own self, or challenging because if you treat everyone with the same low regard that you feel for yourself, it will be no gift to your neighbor. Thankfully, most of us treat ourselves very well. It is not difficult to be kind and charitable to as many people as is humanly possible but sometimes, we are busy with our own challenges and frankly, could use a bit of kindness from someone else. "Be kind" is on the spin cycle in my head. Pick a positive mantra and keep it close to your heart.

Island Mindfulness

I like the 10 Commandments because they have the power to create a better day for all of us. But I challenge you to create an additional five commandments for your life. It is an opportunity to sit quietly, reflect on your life and define for yourself what principles you want to be your guide. There is a wise saying, "Don't be so heavenly bound that you serve no purpose on Earth." Live, love, serve, give, be kind, and speak your truth while you are blessed with life on Earth. Resist the urge to judge others. Judge your own life with kindness, express your beliefs with grace, knowing that we are all a tiny part of the universe and that we have not scratched the surface in exploring all the truths that exist.

PART 5:

Everything Is Irie: Lessons From The Journey

ISLAND MINDFULNESS

"Lean into each moment and let the transformation begin."

ISLAND MINDFULNESS: HOW TO USE THE TRANSFORMATIONAL
POWER OF MINDFULNESS TO CREATE AN ABUNDANT LIFE

www.janetautherine.com

> *"If you are lonely when you are alone, you're in bad company."*
>
> **GRACE JONES**

One Love, One Heart: Navigating Love and Marriage

Love is the most precious gift that the universe offers. For me, an abundant life is one filled with love. When someone offers you love and you accept it, protect their heart. Authentic love begins with self-love. Without self-love, you may be loving for reasons that originate from a place of brokenness, such as, fulfilling a deep need, making up for lack of parental love, filling the void from past hurts, rebounding from an unhealthy relationship, needing to love someone in order to feel useful and worthy, or needing to hide in someone else's shadow. When you know and love yourself, you have a clearer vision of incompatibilities and have the wisdom and courage to say no to someone who may be perfect but not perfect for you. You have the patience to wait for the right one to come along. I am sharing the most important lessons that I have learned on my journey to love.

If you are dating, first know yourself and then know what you want to attract in your life. Write it down. You may not get it all but you won't be blinded by "shiny things" that are sent to distract you from your journey to a fulfilling relationship. Here is an example, but sit with your own thoughts, have a vision of what abundance means for you in a relationship, and create your own. I want to attract someone who is:

1. Emotionally intelligent – in touch with his feelings and emotions and not afraid to express them in a caring and constructive manner.

2. Respects your whole being – loves more than your external beauty and honors your mind, body, spirt and soul.

3. Walks in love and peace – cares for humanity through words and actions. Has a gentle spirit – not quick to start an argument, highlight your imperfections, or break your spirit.

4. Consistently brings his best self – aims for excellence in every area of his life and brings that excellence to the relationship.

5. Caretaker of your inner flame – supports the parts of you that brings you joy. Wants to see you happy, see you achieve your goals and never wants to see that light in your eyes dim.

Self-reflection helps you define what you want in a partner and also helps you to have a keen awareness of what you are able to contribute to a relationship.

If you have found love, you have already been abundantly blessed but making it last can be challenging because we tend to put love on auto-pilot. This is where mindfulness can help the most. On my journey, I have learned to:

1. Never take love for granted. Love can die so treat it like it is fragile even if you know that it is rock solid.

2. Ask questions, listen and get to really know the person that you are with and not your idea of them. You are a stranger to some parts of your spouse or significant other, even if you have been together for many years. In most cases, she has had 25+ years of living before meeting you and there is still many unknowns, even in marriage.

3. Do something kind for your spouse each day. Treat her like your best friend. Bring value to the marriage in the same way that you brought it to the dating relationship.

4. Be intimate daily, even if it is just holding hands. Touch hands, linger and smile when you pass the remote; even the smallest show of affection matters.

5. Be very generous with your words of affirmation. You cannot say, "I love you" enough.

6. If you are a spiritual being, pray for each other each morning. Even if you have had a bad night, you to start each day wishing each other the best.

7. Embrace every opportunity to show kindness. Recognize birthdays, valentine's day and every special occasion. Most of us wouldn't say that Mother's Day is man-made, a waste of money, or that I show love to my mother every day so why recognize her again on mother's day. Treat you significant other with the same regard.

8. Not every disagreement has to be a battle and not every battle has to be won by you. Be mindful of what is really important to you so that you know when to stand your ground and when to walk away.

9. Learn your partner's love language. If her love language is acts of service, showering her with affection or gifts won't harm, but you will get more goodwill from helping her with the chores, not doing the dishes could ruin the marriage.

10. The little things matter. Sweat the small stuff because marriage is made up made of a million small things. When you take care of the small things daily, you may have room to mess up on a big thing occasionally.

11. Substantive conversations are essential. We are not journeying with each other every moment. Most of us don't spend more than two hours of quality time with each other in a 24 hour period. There is a lot of human experiences that are missed and needs to be reflected on and shared. Your spouse is not the same person that you married 10 years ago and if something significant happened at work, she may not be the same person who left the house this morning. What have you learned about yourself this week or this month that you would like to share with your partner?

12. Seek counseling periodically. Don't wait until things are on the verge of falling apart. Your friends can provide wonderful support and a safety net but they are not counselors.

Remember that if you have love, you are already winning in life. That knowledge gives you power to walk in gratitude each day.

Island Mindfulness

If you can, spend a weekend alone and do a self-assessment. Don't judge yourself, just reflect and collect data. Where are you now on your journey? Can you explain that to someone else? Are you comfortable in your own skin? What do you feel is missing in your life? I don't believe that you have to wait until you are perfect to love because that day may never come. I wrote a poem, titled The Art of Loving a Broken Vessel. It states:

THE ART OF LOVING A BROKEN VESSEL

A broken vessel needs love the most
Repair it with gentle hands and a kind heart
Apply patience to the bumps and rough edges
Fill the vulnerable places with love
Turn its broken pieces into perfectly imperfect art
Treasure the masterpiece that you have restored.

Sometimes, we need to be loved both in our darkness and in our light but there has to be self-awareness and honesty. Be mindful of where you are on your journey so that you can bring your true self to a relationship. As you seek, remember that love is a peaceful path and should not be harmful to your mind, body or spirit.

FOLLOW THE LOVE

Follow the love
it is a peaceful path
there is no climbing up dangerous terrain
battling dragons and demons along the way
carefully tiptoeing over hidden land mines

Follow the love
it doesn't hurt
you don't have to change yourself to receive it
it accepts that you are perfectly made
and no permission is needed to travel
confidently in the world

Follow the love
you will recognize it by its non-resistance
its warm embrace
its offer for you to sit awhile
its sheer joy in being found.

> *"One boyfriend told me that I loved myself too much. I thought, well, you can love a boyfriend too much, but you can't love yourself too much. You have to love yourself to keep yourself whole."*
>
> **GRACE JONES**

Self-care is Life-care

Around 2002, I developed a goiter on my neck. It may have been developing for years but that is when it became visible. Over the course of about four years, it grew and became prominent. I resisted all efforts to have it surgically removed. I employed radical self-care, experimented with veganism, ate a diet of raw foods, tried every Jamaican herb, visited several wholistic medicine doctors to explore non-surgical options, while spending thousands of dollars because wholistic treatments were not covered by traditional insurance. I became healthier but the goiter didn't go away. I added exercise and got into the best shape of my life but still it persisted. I have always believed that we are what we eat, so I had to rule out everything that was in my control before surgery.

The thyroid dysfunction was also causing me to have brain fog. I realized that I didn't have the same vivid memory of my childhood as some of my friends, and I often asked my brother to fill in details about our primary school days. In addition to the thyroid goiter, I also developed fibroids. Uterine fibroids are very prevalent in women of African descent. I decided to have a Myomectomy to remove them because I was planning to start a family but a few years later, they returned. There are some hereditary elements to my medical conditions but I believe that they were exacerbated by stress. Most of my life, I was afraid to speak my truth and when I spoke, I didn't even recognize the sound of my own voice. I didn't want to be a disrupter; I just wanted to work hard, go with the flow and avoid the spotlight. I said yes to a lot of things when I should have said no. I didn't allow myself to get angry and when I did, I didn't let the anger out so it stayed in and became toxic. I wrote this poem Fibroids/You are Worthy to remind myself and my sisters that there are health consequences to not speaking your truth, and to absorbing stress.

FIBROIDS/YOU ARE WORTHY

Stress
Unmet expectations
Failure to exhale
Generational toxicity
Swallowing your pride
Hiding your feelings
Saying yes when you mean no

The words and emotions that are unexpressed travel
to bruise the throat,
wound the heart,

pollute the soul
before finding its resting place on and around the uterus
polluting the center of our being
threatening everything in its path.

My sisters, speak your truth
Embrace and love your whole being
Fiercely guard your heart
Be weary of anyone controlling your life in the name
of God, the devil and everything in between.

Clothe yourself in optimism
Banish all forms of negative energy
Take time for mental and physical healthcare
Self-care is Life-care
Proudly recognize that you are the President,
CEO and Keynote Speaker of your life
Nothing important to you works without a healthy you
You are worthy of love, worthy of abundance and
worthy of a healthy life. Always.

Island Mindfulness

Without abundance mentally and physically, it is almost impossible to have abundance in other areas of life. With some exceptions, you have the capacity to mentally build your own prison or build your own paradise. Self-care is a love letter that we write to ourselves and then put into action. Walking around with a goiter taught me to be humble. It felt like no one saw me because they were so busy staring at the goiter. In fact, many didn't even see it but I was carrying a negative narrative in my head that affected how I walked in the world. Not wanting to be a disrupter, just the nice girl with the pretty smile, was affecting both my mental and physical health. I had to be mindful of my entire being. My advice is to care for yourself in the gentle manner that you would care for a precious rose or orchid. Sprinkle kind words throughout your mind. Infuse your body with minerals and vegetation from the earth. Feed your soul with mindfulness and meditation. Fill your spirit with consciousness and unrestrained optimism. Let your spirit be unconstrained by negative energy . Let your voice be heard. If that sounds poetic and lofty, it was meant to be. We are our most precious resource. Self-care is Life-care.

> *"I grew up in poverty and my mother had to sacrifice a lot for us to eat and get an education – just imagine in a house where we were more than six children! But hard work and dedication is what it took for me to be here today."*
>
> **SHELLY-ANN FRASER-PRYCE**

Honoring our Roots: The Strength of a Woman

I was raised by strong Jamaican women, strong because of the circumstance of their birth. They carried water on their heads, farmed the land, raised their babies and the children of others in the community; they worked as many jobs as they could get to make ends meet; they kneeled down to dig yam and climbed trees to pick mango and breadfruit. They didn't have time to be vulnerable. If they cried, the tears were quickly dried because there was work to do.

Children had to be resilient and disciplined because there was no time to coddle anyone, no time to give time-outs or talk through "feelings." Their men were often undisciplined; they could be relied on to work and fix things but they laid their hats at several homes. Point being, you were raised to be tough, to rely on yourself and to solve problems, instead of crying over them. Reflecting on their journey, I wrote this poem.

STRONG. BLACK. WOMAN

Hold on to a shred of dignity.
Scream inside.
Let the tears fall behind closed doors.
You are your mama's child
and she is a proud black woman.

She would be disappointed
if she knew that your heart breaks so easily.
That you blow in the wind
when she raised you to be strong.

Strong. Black. Woman.
Each word is non-negotiable,
so swallow hard,
steady yourself,
and carry on.

I have never enjoyed being referred to as "strong" because it felt like that praise just took away my ability to show any signs of weakness or vulnerability. Many women are strong because they have had to gird their waists and sharpen their edges to survive. Sometimes, the person praising them for being strong was the one causing the challenges. Vulnerability should be a right because it is an intricate part of our humanity, but for many, it was and is a privilege.

Island Mindfulness

Many of us have mothers and grandmothers who have had to sacrifice so that we can be vulnerable, so that we can have a voice in this world. These women are our roots. Speak their names often. Learn their stories even though they may appear to be secretive. That generation believed that what happened in the house stays in the house, and that their lives may not be significant enough to write about. Don't make a fuss but stay close and listen and absorb the bits of wisdom that you will receive. For those that have passed, remember their names and speak their names to children and grandchildren. Mention their names with gratitude in your daily prayer or meditation. Most importantly, gift yourself with the vulnerability and self-care that many of our ancestors could not. I recognize that my ancestors of Caribbean and African descent have already paved the way for me to live an abundant life. The same holds true for you. Remember their stories as you embark on a mindful journey to an abundant life.

STRONG SISTERS UNITE

My sisters, we are standing in the quicksand of political, racial, relationship and other societal dysfunctions Bravely declaring our strength and struggling to hold it together but at what cost We have nothing to prove; let us protect our minds & bodies

Our strength is being used against us
Our ability to be the fixer in every situation masks
our humanity, our femininity, our vulnerability
Let's not wait until we can't breathe to try to escape;
if we delay the healing, our scars will be permanent

The world knows that we are strong because
our strength is legendary
We are Harriet Tubman, Michelle Obama, and Rosa Parks.
We are Oprah Winfrey, Nanny, and Mae Jameson
We are Shirley Chisholm, Portia
Simpson and Maya Angelou
We have birthed a nation, rescued slaves, built empires,
traveled to space and written our place in history

Survival is not enough; we were built to rise
Let us take each other's hand in love and support
Embrace our vulnerabilities
Embrace our humanity
Heal our hearts and minds
Escape from negativity is not failure

> "*Life is one big road with lots of signs. So, when you're riding through the ruts, don't complicate your mind. Flee from hate, mischief, and jealousy. Don't bury your thoughts, put your vision to reality. Wake Up and Live!*"
>
> **BOB MARLEY**

Lessons Learned from Taking the Long, Rugged but Scenic Drive Home

I once told my mother that I acted based on her advice. I actually thought that it would make her happy to hear that I still listened to her and respected her advice. I was surprised to hear her say, "You are a grown woman now; you make your own decisions!" What? When did that happen? In most cases, after reaching 30, your life rests squarely on your own shoulders. The time to blame others—teachers, parents, past significant others—for your problems is long gone. Friends have their own challenges and don't have time for the long heart-to-heart talks that we used to have when we were younger. So, you get your act together and have the confidence to figure it out yourself.

In one of my most challenging years, my father and my beloved cat, Rudy, passed away. I went through the stress of negotiating the purchase of a new house and moving; my family was in a pretty scary car accident that totaled my car, I made an impulse purchase of a new car that wasn't the right fit for our family, and I was blindsided by unnecessary family drama. Life comes with great joys and great disappointments, and you are constantly learning and then being tested. After some soul-searching, here are the top 25 lessons that I have learned over the past 40 years:

1. What I know for sure is that the world is still a mystery, but based on my life experiences, I do have confidence in a few things. I am confident that there is a God and that love and kindness can solve almost every problem that we face.

2. We have to understand the past to make sense of our present. Trace your roots and speak to your elders about their experiences.

3. I am optimistic about life, and sometimes my head is in the clouds. I can live with that; it is pretty up there.

4. You might as well embrace your parents because we either marry a version of our parents or we become them as we get older.

5. Death is final; only our memories remain, so make good memories.

6. When someone that you love dies, you only remember the good times. Try to focus on their good qualities when they are alive.

7. Behind anger and hate are pain and fear. Keep that in mind when you are angry at someone or someone else is angry at you. Try to dig deeper.

8. Not everyone will agree with you; that does not mean that they are wrong. You may be dealing with someone whose reality is just very different from yours.

9. If you lose your way in love, stop, breathe, center yourself and take direction from your heart.

10. Create your own family with the people who consistently show you love through words and deeds.

11. It is possible to feel both love and pain in places within you that you didn't even know existed.

12. We were perfectly made by a wonderful God. We all have a purpose. Our natural tendency is to love; every negative energy is unnatural and will eat away at our souls if we don't let go of it.

13. When you are feeling down, see your way out by helping or inspiring someone else. Don't be judgmental. Be kind and understanding regarding the road that others have traveled

and the path that they have chosen for their lives.

14. Shower God, family, friends, and neighbors with love.

15. Pray every day and always give thanks for your blessings.

16. Contribute to the life of a child that is not your own.

17. Nourish your mind, body, and soul and continue to be open to new truths.

18. Eat real food. We are what we eat.

19. Material things = fleeting happiness. If someone loves something that you own, give it away with a smile.

20. Don't be afraid to feel every emotion (laughter, sadness, tears, joy, and pain). Feel it but don't dwell on it, and don't hide it with substances, (legal or illegal).

21. Religion is hollow if you just send thoughts and prayers and don't lend a hand to your neighbor daily.

22. Strong relationships and strong friendships mean everything. We are our brother's keeper.

23. Be mindful. Take a moment every day through prayer or meditation to listen to what is in your heart.

24. Listen more than you speak and give more than you receive.

25. Exercise every week. Sometimes, that means exercising your facial muscles by smiling at everyone that you meet and exercising your arms by giving everyone a hug.

Island Mindfulness

Every day is another opportunity to learn and grow. We have a wealth of knowledge, and we are blessed with a healthy range of emotions; however, we are just raindrops in the sea of life. Embrace the joys and the disappointments; there is so much more to discover, so never get too discouraged. If you are on a bumpy patch in life, recognize it, own it, and learn all that you can from the experiences—and know that you have survived challenges in the past and will continue to be a survivor. Finally, share your experiences because, although we may feel alone, we are never truly alone. Your experiences can be the beacon of light that someone needs not to stumble on their journey. Every footprint that you leave in the sand can be your legacy of strength, struggle, and hope.

"Power through. If you lose your way, follow the footsteps in the sand. If you stumble, angels are ready to hold your hand. If you fall, God will carry you to your destination."

The Beginning and the End

HEAVENLY FATHER

When I walked alone
You took my hand and held it gently
You provided a steady shoulder to cry on
You said that all would be well,
but I didn't believe you so
You took my life into your hands

My first day of school, you held my hand
as I walked through the doors
When the teacher smiled at me, I thanked you
When a kid sat next to me at lunch, my heart thanked you
Maybe everything would be fine

When a bully made fun of my nose,
you reminded me that I am perfect
You sent your angel to accompany me
When I lost a race, you reminded me that
I am a winner in your eyes

When I didn't fit in, you told me that sometimes
it was ok to stand out

I graduated from high school today and
I am not sure what the future holds
In my uncertainty, I prayed for your guidance
You led me to follow my heart
You promised that whatever path I choose,
you would be by my side

I went off to college today, but before I left,
I looked up and prayed
There were some wild times and some somber times
I lost my way a few times, but you never left me
You just silently surrounded me with your protection

I was never without a heavenly Father
You have never let me down
There was no need to find myself;
you always assured me that I was
your child. I stood firmly in your shadow

Today, I received a diploma that
sends me out into the world
You smiled down at me
I turn my head towards heaven and give you a high-five
As I go into the world, I know that I am on my own,
but I am never alone.

Island Mindfulness

What we know for sure is that there was a beginning and there will be an end. In most cases, we are not in control of either ends; however, we can be mindful of the dash in between. This book is an encouragement to be mindful of your journey and live a meaningful life in accordance with your own terms. Live in a space of gratitude and show appreciation for the experiences that shape you and the people that have added meaning to your life. I end with the poem Heavenly Father, which I wrote while reflecting on my journey during my formative years. God was with me then and has been with me every step of the way and I am eternally grateful.

EPILOGUE: The Poetry of Life – A Cottage on a Hill in Jamaica Overlooking the Ocean

Owning a cottage on a hill overlooking the ocean in Jamaica is my dream. I would love to awake every morning to a splendid view of the ocean, a cup of tea or Jamaican Blue Mountain coffee, and a plate of tropical fruit. What are you dreaming of? Envision it, vocalize it, write it down, and live as much of it as you can. It is not time to retire, but I sometimes mentally place myself in that atmosphere when I sit to write a story or a poem. Live in the present but don't give up on your dreams.

My story is not complete without poetry. I lead with my heart and all the thoughts that won't easily flow from my introvert brain, flow easily on paper. When I sit to write a poem, I drown out all the noise of the world and focus on just the thoughts and emotions of the moment. This is when I can truly be in a space of mindfulness. My love for poetry started around age eight while I was still living in Jamaica and even today, I find that I am most creative when sitting on the beach—whether on an island or on one of the many beaches in Florida. I have taken many solo trips to the beaches in Clearwater and Sarasota to meditate and write. Island mindfulness is a mindset that you can take with you wherever your journey takes you.

Quiet reflection and writing have been my tools for living in the moment but also my bridge for getting to the other side when everything did not feel Irie. The beauty of poetry is the ability of the reader to interpret each word through their own lens, so I won't add commentary on mindful living. In 2018, I was blessed to publish my first book of poems, Wild Heart, Peaceful Soul (available on Amazon). I will leave you with a poem that is the root of my island mindfulness journey.

CHILD OF JAMAICA

Jamaica saved me
reminded me that
heritage matters
pride matters
respect matters
child of strength
child of peace
child out of many one people
stand tall
reach high
practice one love
your ancestors
are watching

Thanks for taking the time to read about my journey through stories and poetry. Let's raise a glass of coconut water to a purposeful, abundant and Irie life.

About The Author

Janet Autherine was born in the small town of Dalvey in the Parrish of St. Thomas, Jamaica, and immigrated to the United States when she was twelve. She grew up in Philadelphia and received her undergraduate degree from Pennsylvania State University and her law degree from Boston College Law School. After establishing her legal career in Washington, D.C., as a tax attorney and an administrative law judge, she was eventually drawn back to the sunshine and now lives in Florida with her three sons.

The beauty of island life in Jamaica, as well as the struggles, defined her formative years and have guided every aspect of her life and career. She is an author, poet, and proud introvert, who created Autherine Publishing and the Growing into Greatness series of books, poetry, and blog posts to provide inspiration and empower. Embrace your humanity, embrace the greatness that is within you, and leave footprints in the sand to guide the next generation.

Other books by Janet Autherine: *Growing into Greatness with God: 7 Paths to Greatness for our Sons and Daughters* and the women's empowerment book *Wild Heart, Peaceful Soul: Reclaiming your Heart in Order to Live and Love Harmoniously.* You can find her work at www.JanetAutherine.com.

Moment Of Gratitude

This book is dedicated to my wonderful circle of friends and family who have loved and supported me and have kept me sane and in a state of "island mindfulness" during challenging times. My sons, Gabriel, Giorgio, and Gian—you bring me immeasurable joy and remind me every day to focus on what is important in life. Much love to my wonderful mother, Roslyn Chambers and brother, Mark Walker, who have been my solid rocks and my sisters, Donna and Odene, who give me continuous love and support. To my circle of friends and writing cheerleaders, your love and encouragement mean everything to me. Special thanks to my guardian angel, Linett Wills, whose prayers still guide me. I love you all.

Definitions

ISLAND: a tract of land surrounded by water; an isolated group or area. (Merriam-Webster)

MINDFULNESS: the energy of being aware and awake to the present moment. It is the continuous practice of touching life deeply in every moment of daily life. To be mindful is to be truly alive, present, and at one with those around you and with what you are doing. We bring our body and mind into harmony while we wash the dishes, drive the car, or take our morning shower. (Thich Nhat Hanh Foundation)

IRIE: to be at total peace with your current state of being. The way you feel when you have no worries, you are feeling good and living in harmony. (Urban dictionary)

ISLAND MINDFULNESS: island mindfulness is the awareness that each of us is a small but significant voice in the world and that the world needs us to have the peace of mind to live and love harmoniously. Although we may be surrounded by water (literally or figuratively), the mind has the ability to ride the waves of life and find calm in the midst of all the sun, wind, and rain that will touch our lives. By focusing on mindful living and being, the mind, heart, and soul can be Irie (at peace).

Acknowledgement

I have included quotes from some of the reggae legends that I grew up listening to in Jamaica, as well as leaders who have inspired me. I have a deep love for reggae music because the beat is the heartbeat of Jamaica and the lyrics tell the story of the people. Attribution given to the Honorable Robert Nesta Marley, Peter Tosh, Jimmy Cliff, Marcus Garvey, Usain Bolt, the Honorable Portia Simpson-Miller, Louise Bennett, Grace Jones, and Shelly-Ann Fraser-Pryce. Deepest gratitude to all the leaders that continue to inspire us to be our best selves.

www.ingramcontent.com/pod-product-compliance
Lightning Source LLC
LaVergne TN
LVHW051523070426
835507LV00023B/3263